M000250810

SMALL PLATES

Small Plates

Copyright © 2021 by Appleseed Press Book Publishers LLC.

This is an officially licensed book by Cider Mill Press Book Publishers LLC.

All rights reserved under the Pan-American and International Copyright Conventions.

No part of this book may be reproduced in whole or in part, scanned, photocopied, recorded, distributed in any printed or electronic form, or reproduced in any manner whatsoever, or by any information storage and retrieval system now known or hereafter invented, without express written permission of the publisher, except in the case of brief quotations embodied in critical articles and reviews.

The scanning, uploading, and distribution of this book via the Internet or via any other means without permission of the publisher is illegal and punishable by law. Please support authors' rights, and do not participate in or encourage piracy of copyrighted materials.

13-Digit ISBN: 978-1-64643-145-8
10-Digit ISBN: 1-64643-145-6

This book may be ordered by mail from the publisher. Please include $5.99 for postage and handling. Please support your local bookseller first!

Books published by Cider Mill Press Book Publishers are available at special discounts for bulk purchases in the United States by corporations, institutions, and other organizations. For more information, please contact the publisher.

Cider Mill Press Book Publishers
"Where good books are ready for press"

PO Box 454
12 Spring Street
Kennebunkport, Maine 04046

Visit us online!
cidermillpress.com

Typography: Brandon Grotesque, Operetta

Photos on 22, 45, 46, 55, 59, 64, 67, 71, 91, 96, 100, 103, 129, 137, 142, 162, 166, 170, 177, 187, 191, 199, 204, 208, 211, 212, 219, 228, and 232 courtesy of Cider Mill Press. All other photos used under official license from Shutterstock.com.

Front endpaper image: Savory Tart Shells, see page 57
Back endpaper image: Stuffed Mushrooms, see page 151

Printed in China

1 2 3 4 5 6 7 8 9 0

First Edition

OVER 100 IDEAS

SMALL PLATES

FOR BITES AND NIBBLES

CIDER MILL
PRESS

BOOK
PUBLISHERS
KENNEBUNKPORT, MAINE

Chicken Souvlaki, page 185

CONTENTS

INTRODUCTION

Peppers Stuffed with Greek Salad, page 132

Following a brief surge of popularity, the concept of "small plates" has suffered some in recent years, as many diners became sick of walking away from a table with their wallets lighter than ever and sans the satisfaction one expects from such expenditures. Indeed, some restaurateurs have pushed the concept in an attempt to line their pockets, while others have fallen under the spell of social media, and chosen to emphasize style over substance.

These misguided few have obscured what a wonderful option a meal consisting of various small dishes is for the gourmet in the fast-paced modern world. By doing little more than picking up a loaf of bread, a nice wedge of cheese, and a cured meat or two on your way home and flanking them with easy-to-make sauces, dips, and salads made from the odds and ends in your kitchen, an enjoyable meal becomes easily available.

The small plate approach is also often the best option for a get-together with friends and family. Instead of flipping through food blogs, websites, and cookbooks for a recipe that accomplishes the impossible task of satisfying and impressing all, a spread consisting of numerous bites allows everyone to find something to their liking, whether they be vegetarian, gluten-free, or pure carnivore.

Hummus, page 43

SAUCES, DIPS
& SPREADS

A good meal can be as simple as drizzling freshly made pesto over a piece of mozzarella, going out to the garden, picking a few ripe tomatoes from the vine, and whipping up some salsa, or covering a few toasted pieces of bread with a schmear of something decadent and a few thinly sliced raw vegetables.

The preparations in this chapter bring this pleasing simplicity within reach of all, and provide the bold cook with myriad opportunities to transform the dishes in the other chapters.

BASIL PESTO

YIELD: **1 CUP** / ACTIVE TIME: **10 MINUTES** / TOTAL TIME: **25 MINUTES**

INGREDIENTS

¼ cup pine nuts

3 garlic cloves

Salt and pepper, to taste

2 cups firmly packed fresh basil leaves

½ cup extra-virgin olive oil

¼ cup grated Parmesan cheese

1 teaspoon fresh lemon juice

1   Warm a small skillet over low heat for 1 minute. Add the pine nuts and cook, while shaking the pan, until they begin to give off a toasty fragrance, 2 to 3 minutes. Transfer to a plate and let cool completely.

2   Place the garlic, salt, and pine nuts in a food processor or blender and pulse until the mixture is a coarse meal. Add the basil and pulse it is until finely minced. Transfer the mixture to a medium bowl and, while whisking to incorporate, add the oil in a slow stream.

3   Add the cheese and stir until thoroughly incorporated. Stir in the lemon juice, taste, and adjust the seasoning as necessary. The pesto will keep in the refrigerator for up to 2 days.

NOTE: You can also make this pesto using a mortar and pestle, which will give it more texture.

MIGNONETTE SAUCE

YIELD: **6 SERVINGS** / ACTIVE TIME: **5 MINUTES** / TOTAL TIME: **5 MINUTES**

INGREDIENTS

1½ tablespoons minced shallot

⅓ cup white vinegar

½ teaspoon crushed black pepper

Salt, to taste

1 Place all of the ingredients in a small bowl and stir to combine.

HARISSA SAUCE

YIELD: 1½ CUPS / ACTIVE TIME: **25 MINUTES** / TOTAL TIME: **35 MINUTES**

INGREDIENTS

1 habanero pepper

¾ teaspoon caraway seeds

¾ teaspoon coriander seeds

1½ teaspoons cumin seeds

1½ teaspoons dried mint

1 tablespoon kosher salt, plus more to taste

12 garlic cloves

Juice of 3 lemons

3 tablespoons extra-virgin olive oil

1 cup plain, full-fat Greek yogurt

1 teaspoon finely chopped fresh cilantro

1 teaspoon finely chopped fresh mint

1 teaspoon finely chopped fresh parsley

1 teaspoon finely chopped fresh chives

Black pepper, to taste

1   Hold the habanero over an open flame on your stove or under the broiler. Roast, while turning, until all sides of the pepper are charred. Place the pepper in a bowl, cover it with plastic wrap, and let it sit for 10 minutes. Remove the stem, skin, and seeds from the pepper (gloves are recommended while handling the habanero) and discard them. Mince the habanero's flesh and set it aside.

2   Place the seeds in a dry skillet and toast them over medium heat, shaking the pan frequently, until the seeds begin to release their aroma. Remove the seeds from the pan and let them cool. When cool, grind the seeds into a fine powder, using either a spice grinder or a mortar and pestle.

3   Place the remaining ingredients, the roasted habanero, and the toasted seed powder in a food processor, blitz until smooth, and use as desired.

ROMESCO SAUCE

YIELD: **1 CUP** / ACTIVE TIME: **5 MINUTES** / TOTAL TIME: **5 MINUTES**

INGREDIENTS

2 large red bell peppers, roasted

1 garlic clove, smashed

½ cup slivered almonds, toasted

¼ cup tomato puree

2 tablespoons chopped
fresh parsley

2 tablespoons sherry vinegar

1 teaspoon smoked paprika

Salt and pepper, to taste

½ cup extra-virgin olive oil

1   Place all of the ingredients, except for the olive oil, in a blender or food processor and pulse until the mixture is smooth. Transfer the sauce to a mixing bowl.

2   Add the olive oil in a slow stream and whisk until emulsified. Season with salt and pepper and use immediately.

ROASTED TOMATO SALSA

YIELD: **1 CUP** / ACTIVE TIME: **20 MINUTES** / TOTAL TIME: **2 HOURS**

INGREDIENTS

1 lb. ripe tomatoes, cored and halved

1½ teaspoons extra-virgin olive oil

Salt and pepper, to taste

2 tablespoons minced yellow onion

½ jalapeño pepper, stemmed, seeded, and minced

1 tablespoon chopped fresh cilantro

1 tablespoon fresh lime juice

1   Preheat your oven to 450°F. Place the tomatoes, olive oil, salt, and pepper in a large bowl and toss to coat. Let stand for 30 minutes.

2   Place the tomatoes, cut side down, on a baking sheet, place them in the oven, and roast until they start to char and soften, about 10 minutes. Carefully turn the tomatoes over and roast until they start bubbling, about 5 minutes. Remove from the oven and let the tomatoes cool completely.

3   Chop the tomatoes and place them in a bowl with the remaining ingredients. Stir to combine and let stand at room temperature for 45 minutes. Taste, adjust seasoning if necessary, and serve. The salsa will keep in the refrigerator for up to 2 days.

SALSA VERDE

YIELD: **1 CUP** / ACTIVE TIME: **5 MINUTES** / TOTAL TIME: **15 MINUTES**

INGREDIENTS

6 tomatillos, husked and
rinsed well

8 serrano peppers, stemmed and
seeded to taste

½ yellow onion, chopped

2 garlic cloves, minced

Salt, to taste

¼ cup extra-virgin olive oil

Fresh cilantro, chopped,
for garnish

1 Place the tomatillos and serrano peppers in a large
saucepan and cover with water. Bring to a boil and cook
until the tomatillos start to lose their bright green color,
about 10 minutes.

2 Drain and transfer the tomatillos and peppers to a
blender. Add all of the remaining ingredients, except
for the cilantro, and puree until smooth. Top with the
cilantro and serve. The salsa will keep in the refrigerator
for up to 2 days.

BACON JAM

YIELD: **6 SERVINGS** / ACTIVE TIME: **40 MINUTES** / TOTAL TIME: **1 HOUR AND 30 MINUTES**

INGREDIENTS

1½ lbs. bacon

2 teaspoons unsalted butter

4 yellow onions, chopped

1 teaspoon kosher salt

¼ cup brown sugar

¼ cup sherry vinegar

1½ teaspoons fresh thyme leaves

1 teaspoon black pepper

Pinch of cayenne pepper

½ cup water

2 teaspoons balsamic vinegar

2 teaspoons extra-virgin olive oil

1 Place the bacon in a large saucepan and cook over medium heat and cook until crispy, about 10 minutes. Working over a heatproof bowl, strain the bacon and its rendered fat. Let the bacon drain and cool. When all of the fat has been drained and the bacon is cool enough to handle, finely chop the bacon.

2 Place the saucepan over medium heat and add the butter and 2 teaspoons of the reserved bacon fat. When the butter begins to foam, add the onions and salt and cook, stirring frequently, until the onions are soft, about 10 minutes. Stir in the brown sugar, sherry vinegar, 1 teaspoon of thyme leaves, the black pepper, cayenne, water, and the bacon. Cook until the mixture is brick red in color and has a jammy consistency, about 10 minutes.

3 Remove the pan from heat and stir in the balsamic vinegar, olive oil, and remaining thyme. Let cool before serving.

ROASTED ARTICHOKE & SPINACH DIP

YIELD: **1 CUP** / ACTIVE TIME: **5 MINUTES** / TOTAL TIME: **15 MINUTES**

INGREDIENTS

¾ lb. artichoke hearts, quartered

4 garlic cloves, unpeeled

2 cups baby spinach

2 tablespoons apple cider vinegar

¼ teaspoon kosher salt

¼ cup extra-virgin olive oil

Pinch of onion powder (optional)

1   Preheat the oven's broiler to high. Place the artichoke hearts and garlic on a baking sheet and broil, turning them occasionally, until browned all over, about 10 minutes. Remove from the oven and let cool. When cool enough to handle, peel the garlic cloves.

2   Place the artichoke hearts and garlic in a food processor, add the remaining ingredients, and blitz until the desired texture for the spread is achieved.

GREEN GODDESS DIP

YIELD: **6 CUPS** / ACTIVE TIME: **5 MINUTES** / TOTAL TIME: **5 MINUTES**

INGREDIENTS

1½ cups mayonnaise

2 cups sour cream

1 tablespoon chopped fresh
parsley

1 tablespoon chopped fresh
tarragon

1 tablespoon chopped fresh
chives

1 tablespoon chopped fresh basil

1 tablespoon red wine vinegar

1 tablespoon sugar

1 teaspoon garlic powder

1 tablespoon Worcestershire
sauce

Salt and pepper, to taste

6 oz. blue cheese

1   Place all of the ingredients, except for the blue cheese, in a food processor and blitz until pureed.

2   Add the blue cheese and pulse a few times, making sure to maintain a chunky texture. Store in the refrigerator until ready to serve.

WHITE BEAN & ROSEMARY SPREAD

YIELD: **2 CUPS** / ACTIVE TIME: **5 MINUTES** / TOTAL TIME: **35 MINUTES**

INGREDIENTS

1 (14 oz.) can of cannellini beans,
drained and rinsed

2 tablespoons extra-virgin
olive oil

2 teaspoons balsamic vinegar

2 garlic cloves, minced

1 tablespoon chopped
fresh rosemary

½ celery stalk, peeled
and minced

Salt and pepper, to taste

2 pinches of red pepper flakes

1   Place half of the beans in a bowl and mash them. Add
the rest of the beans, the olive oil, vinegar, garlic,
rosemary, and celery and stir to combine.

2   Season with salt, pepper, and red pepper flakes and
cover the bowl with plastic wrap. Let stand for about 30
minutes before serving.

ROASTED PUMPKIN DIP

YIELD: **6 TO 8 SERVINGS** / ACTIVE TIME: **5 MINUTES** / TOTAL TIME: **1 HOUR**

INGREDIENTS

1 (3 lb.) sugar pumpkin, halved and seeded

5 tablespoons extra-virgin olive oil

2 teaspoons kosher salt

1 teaspoon black pepper

1 teaspoon chopped fresh thyme

¼ teaspoon freshly grated nutmeg

¼ cup grated Parmesan cheese

1 tablespoon fresh lemon juice

1 tablespoon plain, full-fat Greek yogurt

1   Preheat the oven to 425°F. Place the pumpkin, cut side up, on a parchment-lined baking sheet and brush it with 1 tablespoon of the olive oil. Sprinkle half of the salt over the pumpkin, place it in the oven, and roast for 35 minutes, until the flesh is tender. Remove from the oven and let the pumpkin cool.

2   When the pumpkin is cool enough to handle, scrape the flesh into a food processor. Add the remaining ingredients and puree until smooth.

CRÈME FRAÎCHE

YIELD: **1 CUP** / ACTIVE TIME: **5 MINUTES** / TOTAL TIME: **12 HOURS**

INGREDIENTS

1 cup heavy cream

1 tablespoon buttermilk

1   Place the ingredients in a mason jar, cover it, and let it stand at room temperature for 12 hours. Use immediately or store in the refrigerator for up to 1 month.

GUACAMOLE

YIELD: **2 CUPS** / ACTIVE TIME: **5 MINUTES** / TOTAL TIME: **5 MINUTES**

INGREDIENTS

2 tablespoons chopped red onion

Zest and juice of 1 lime

Salt, to taste

1 jalapeño pepper, stemmed,
seeded, and minced

Flesh from 3 avocados, chopped

2 tablespoons chopped fresh
cilantro

1 plum tomato, peeled, seeded,
and chopped

1   Place the onion, lime zest and juice, salt, and jalapeño in
a mixing bowl and stir to combine.

2   Add the avocados and work the mixture with a fork
until the desired consistency has been reached. Add the
cilantro and tomato, stir to incorporate, and taste. Adjust
seasoning as necessary and serve immediately.

CILANTRO CHUTNEY

YIELD: **6 SERVINGS** / ACTIVE TIME: **5 MINUTES** / TOTAL TIME: **5 MINUTES**

INGREDIENTS

1 bunch of fresh cilantro

¼ cup grated fresh coconut

15 fresh mint leaves

1 tablespoon minced chili pepper

1 garlic clove

1 teaspoon grated fresh ginger

1 plum tomato, peeled, seeded,
and chopped

1 tablespoon fresh lemon juice

Water, as needed

Salt, to taste

1   Place all of the ingredients, except for the water and salt, in a food processor and puree until smooth, adding water as needed to get the desired consistency. Season with salt and store in the refrigerator until ready to serve.

BABA GANOUSH

YIELD: **8 SERVINGS** / ACTIVE TIME: **10 MINUTES** / TOTAL TIME: **45 MINUTES**

INGREDIENTS

1 lb. eggplant

2 garlic cloves, chopped

¼ cup tahini

½ teaspoon fresh lemon juice

1 teaspoon kosher salt

½ teaspoon cumin

½ teaspoon paprika

¼ teaspoon cayenne pepper

2 tablespoons extra-virgin olive oil

Fresh parsley, chopped, for garnish

1   Preheat the oven to 400°F. Pierce the skin of the eggplant with a knife or fork and place it on a baking sheet. Place it in the oven and roast for about 35 minutes, until the skin is blistered and the flesh is tender. Remove from the oven and let cool.

2   Peel the eggplant and chop the flesh. Place it in a bowl with the remaining ingredients, except for the parsley, and stir to combine. Garnish with the parsley and serve.

NOTE: For a creamier texture, use a food processor to puree the eggplant before incorporating the rest of the ingredients.

TAPENADE

YIELD: **1½ CUPS** / ACTIVE TIME: **5 MINUTES** / TOTAL TIME: **5 MINUTES**

INGREDIENTS

1½ cups cured olives, pitted

1 teaspoon white miso paste

3 tablespoons capers, rinsed

1½ tablespoons chopped
fresh parsley

3 garlic cloves

3 tablespoons fresh lemon juice

¼ teaspoon black pepper, plus
more to taste

¼ cup extra-virgin olive oil

Salt, to taste

1 Place the olives, miso paste, capers, parsley, garlic, lemon juice, and black pepper in a food processor and pulse the mixture until coarsely chopped.

2 Drizzle the olive oil into the mixture and pulse a few more times until a chunky paste forms, scraping down the work bowl as needed. Season with salt and pepper and serve.

HUMMUS VARIATIONS

For a more authentic hummus, soak dried chickpeas overnight and then cook them in simmering water until tender, about 2 hours. You can also dress the mixture up with any of the following options: add 1 to 3 teaspoons of spices like cumin, sumac, harissa, or smoked paprika; blend in 1 cup of roasted eggplant, zucchini, bell peppers, or garlic; or fold in ¾ cup of chopped olives.

HUMMUS

YIELD: **1½ CUPS** / ACTIVE TIME: **15 MINUTES** / TOTAL TIME: **15 MINUTES**

INGREDIENTS

1 (14 oz.) can of chickpeas

3 tablespoons extra-virgin olive oil

3 tablespoons tahini

1½ tablespoons fresh lemon juice, plus more to taste

1 garlic clove, chopped

1 teaspoon kosher salt

½ teaspoon black pepper

1   Drain the chickpeas and reserve the liquid. If time allows, remove the skins from each of the chickpeas. This will make your hummus much smoother.

2   Place all of the ingredients in a food processor and blitz until the mixture is very smooth, scraping down the work bowl as needed.

3   Taste and adjust the seasoning. If your hummus is stiffer than you'd like, add 2 to 3 tablespoons of the reserved chickpea liquid and blitz until it is the desired consistency.

SMOKED SWEET POTATO PUREE

YIELD: **8 SERVINGS** / ACTIVE TIME: **15 MINUTES** / TOTAL TIME: **1 HOUR AND 15 MINUTES**

INGREDIENTS

½ cup wood chips

2 sweet potatoes, peeled and chopped

1 Yukon Gold potato, peeled and chopped

2 teaspoons kosher salt, plus more to taste

½ cup heavy cream

2 tablespoons unsalted butter

1   Preheat the oven to 250°F. Place the wood chips in a cast-iron skillet and place the pan over high heat. When the wood chips start to smoke, place the skillet in a deep roasting pan. Set the sweet potatoes and potato in the roasting pan (not in the skillet) and cover the roasting pan with aluminum foil. Place in the oven for 30 minutes.

2   While the potatoes are smoking in the oven, bring water to a boil in a large saucepan. Remove all of the potatoes from the oven, salt the boiling water, and add the potatoes. Cook until they are fork-tender, 20 to 25 minutes. Drain, place in a mixing bowl, and add the remaining ingredients. Mash until smooth and serve immediately.

PORK PÂTÉ

YIELD: **10 SERVINGS** / ACTIVE TIME: **20 MINUTES** / TOTAL TIME: **24 HOURS**

INGREDIENTS

3- to 5-lb., bone-in pork shoulder

3 onions, sliced

2 teaspoons ground cloves

1 tablespoon kosher salt, plus more to taste

4 bay leaves

2 teaspoons black pepper, plus more to taste

1 teaspoon freshly grated nutmeg

1   Preheat the oven to 300°F. Place all of the ingredients in a Dutch oven and stir to combine. Cover, place in the oven, and cook until the pork is extremely tender, about 3 to 4 hours.

2   Remove from the oven, discard the bay leaves, and transfer the pork shoulder to a plate. When the pork shoulder has cooled slightly, shred it with a fork.

3   Place the shredded pork and ½ cup of the cooking liquid in a blender. Puree until it forms a paste, adding more cooking liquid as needed to get the desired consistency.

4   Season with salt and pepper, transfer the paste to a large jar, and pour the remaining cooking liquid over it. Cover the jar and store it in the refrigerator overnight before serving.

CHICKEN LIVER MOUSSE

YIELD: **6 SERVINGS** / ACTIVE TIME: **30 MINUTES** / TOTAL TIME: **3 HOURS AND 30 MINUTES**

INGREDIENTS

1 tablespoon unsalted butter

½ lb. chicken liver, chopped

2 tablespoons chopped white onion

1 teaspoon kosher salt

1 teaspoon black pepper

2 tablespoons balsamic vinegar

3 oz. heavy cream

1   Place the butter in a large skillet and melt it over medium-high heat. When the butter begins to foam, add the liver, onion, salt, and pepper and cook, stirring frequently, until liver is no longer pink, about 8 minutes.

2   Transfer the mixture to a food processor and puree. With the food processor running, slowly add the balsamic vinegar. When all of the vinegar has been incorporated, slowly add the cream and puree until smooth.

3   Transfer the mixture to a container, place in the refrigerator, and chill, uncovered, for 1 hour.

4   Cover the continue and refrigerate for another 2 hours, or until the mousse is set.

5   Serve with crackers or grilled bread.

Pita Bread, page 65

BREADS & CRACKERS

There's a contingent of people who would never think of making their own bread or crackers, preferring to trust the famously tricky work of handling dough to the talented artisans who have elected to devote their lives to that task.

The recipes in this chapter target this reticent bunch, providing easy, no-frills preparations that allow you to place a warm, pillowy focaccia or versatile pita beside the other bites you've selected. There's also a simple tart shell, several recipes that'll help you use up the just-past-prime ends of a loaf, and so much more.

NO-KNEAD BREAD

YIELD: **1 LOAF** / ACTIVE TIME: **30 MINUTES** / TOTAL TIME: **24 HOURS**

INGREDIENTS

15.1 oz. (3 cups) all-purpose flour, plus more as needed

¼ teaspoon instant yeast

1¼ teaspoons fine sea salt

13.75 oz. (1½ cups plus 2 tablespoons) water

1   Combine the flour, yeast, and salt in a large mixing bowl. Add the water and stir until a shaggy and sticky dough forms. Cover the bowl with plastic wrap and let the dough rest at room temperature (70°F is ideal) for 18 hours.

2   The next day, the surface of the dough should be dotted with bubbles. Place the dough on a flour-dusted work surface, sprinkle it with a little bit of flour, and fold it over on itself once or twice. Cover the dough loosely with plastic wrap and let rest about 15 minutes.

3   Dust your hands with flour and quickly shape the dough into a ball. Dust a thin cotton towel with flour, place the dough on the towel, seam side down, and cover with another cotton towel. Let the dough sit at room temperature until it has doubled in size and does not eagerly spring back when poked with a finger, about 2 hours.

4   Approximately 30 minutes before the dough will be ready, place a Dutch oven in the oven and preheat the oven to 450°F. When dough is ready, carefully remove pot from oven. Slide your hand under the dough and turn it into the pot, seam side up. Shake to evenly distribute the dough, cover the pot, and place it in the oven. Bake for 30 minutes, remove the lid, and bake until the bread is a beautiful golden brown, 15 to 30 minutes. Remove from the oven and let the bread cool on a wire rack.

CORNBREAD

YIELD: **16 SERVINGS** / ACTIVE TIME: **40 MINUTES** / TOTAL TIME: **2 HOURS AND 15 MINUTES**

INGREDIENTS

5 ears of corn, silk removed

10 tablespoons unsalted butter

1 onion, chopped

2 garlic cloves, minced

2 teaspoons kosher salt, plus
more to taste

2¾ cups heavy cream

2 cups all-purpose flour

2 cups cornmeal

¼ cup brown sugar

2 teaspoons baking powder

½ teaspoon cayenne pepper

½ teaspoon paprika

1½ cups honey

6 eggs

¼ cup sour cream

1   Preheat the oven to 350°F. Place the ears of corn on a baking sheet, place it in the oven, and bake for 25 minutes, until the kernels have a slight give to them. Remove from the oven and let cool. When the ears of corn are cool enough to handle, remove the husks and cut the kernels from the cob. Reserve the corn cobs for another preparation. Lower the oven temperature to 300°F.

2   Place 2 tablespoons of the butter in a large saucepan and melt over medium heat. Add the onion and garlic, season with salt, and cook until the onion is translucent, about 3 minutes. Set ¾ cup of the corn kernels aside and add the rest to the pan. Add 2 cups of the cream and half of the salt and cook until the corn is very tender, about 15 to 20 minutes.

3   Strain, reserve the cream, and transfer the solids to the blender. Puree until smooth, adding the cream as needed if the mixture is too thick. Season to taste and allow the puree to cool completely.

4   Place the flour, cornmeal, remaining salt, brown sugar, baking powder, cayenne pepper, and paprika in a large mixing bowl and stir until combined. Place 2 cups of the corn puree, the honey, eggs, remaining cream, and sour cream in a separate large mixing bowl and stir until combined. Gradually add the dry mixture to the wet mixture and stir to combine. When all of the wet mixture has been incorporated, add the reserved corn kernels and fold the mixture until they are evenly distributed.

5   Grease an 11 x 7–inch baking pan and pour the batter into it. Place the pan in the oven and bake until a toothpick inserted into the center of the cornbread comes out clean, about 35 minutes. Remove from the oven and let it cool briefly before cutting.

SAVORY TART SHELLS

YIELD: **2 TART SHELLS** / ACTIVE TIME: **30 MINUTES** / TOTAL TIME: **2 HOURS**

INGREDIENTS

2½ cups all-purpose flour,
plus more as needed

⅓ cup extra-virgin olive oil

½ cup ice water

1 teaspoon fine sea salt

1   Place all of the ingredients in a bowl and work the mixture until a dough forms. Divide the dough into two pieces, flatten them into disks, wrap them in plastic, and refrigerate for 1 hour.

2   Preheat the oven to 400°F. Grease and flour two 9-inch pie plates. Place the pieces of dough on a flour-dusted work surface and roll them out into ¼-inch-thick rounds. Lay the crusts in the pan, trim any excess away, and prick the bottom of the crusts with a fork or a knife. Cover the crusts with aluminum foil, fill the foil with uncooked rice, dried beans, or pie weights, and place in the oven. Bake until firm and golden brown, about 20 minutes.

3   Remove from the oil, remove the foil and beans, and fill as desired.

NOTE: If not using right away, store in the refrigerator for up to 1 week or in the freezer for up to 6 months.

PANZANELLA
WITH WHITE BALSAMIC VINAIGRETTE

YIELD: **6 SERVINGS** / ACTIVE TIME: **25 MINUTES** / TOTAL TIME: **45 MINUTES**

INGREDIENTS

FOR THE SALAD

1 tablespoon kosher salt, plus 2 teaspoons

6 pearl onions, trimmed

1 cup corn kernels

1 cup chopped green beans

4 cups chopped day-old bread

2 cups chopped overripe tomatoes

10 large fresh basil leaves, torn

Black pepper, to taste

FOR THE VINAIGRETTE

½ cup white balsamic vinegar

¼ cup extra-virgin olive oil

2 tablespoons minced shallot

¼ cup sliced scallions

2 tablespoons chopped fresh parsley

2 teaspoons kosher salt

1 teaspoon black pepper

1   To begin preparations for the salad, bring water to a boil in a small saucepan and prepare an ice water bath. When the water is boiling, add the 1 tablespoon of salt and the pearl onions and cook for 5 minutes. When the onions have 1 minute left to cook, add the corn and green beans to the saucepan. Transfer the vegetables to the ice water bath and let cool completely.

2   Remove the pearl onions from the water bath and squeeze to remove the bulbs from their skins. Cut the bulbs in half and break them down into individual petals. Drain the corn and green beans and pat the vegetables dry.

3   To prepare the vinaigrette, place all of the ingredients in a mixing bowl and whisk until combined.

4   Place the cooked vegetables, bread, tomatoes, and basil in a salad bowl and toss to combine. Add the remaining salt, season with pepper, and add half of the vinaigrette. Toss to coat, taste, and add more of the vinaigrette if desired.

FETT'UNTA

YIELD: **4 SERVINGS** / ACTIVE TIME: **10 MINUTES** / TOTAL TIME: **30 MINUTES**

INGREDIENTS

4 slices from loaf of crusty bread (each slice 1½ inches thick)

¾ cup quality extra-virgin olive oil, plus more as needed

1 garlic clove

Flaky sea salt, to taste

1   Preheat your gas or charcoal grill to high heat. Brush both sides of each slice of bread generously with olive oil.

2   Place the bread on the grill and cook until crisp and browned on both sides, about 2 minutes per side. Remove from heat, rub the garlic clove over one side of each piece, and pour 3 tablespoons of oil over each one. Sprinkle salt over the oil and serve.

FOCACCIA GENOVESE

YIELD: **8 SERVINGS** / ACTIVE TIME: **2 HOURS** / TOTAL TIME: **27 HOURS**

INGREDIENTS

FOR THE DOUGH

15.2 oz. water

¼ teaspoon active dry yeast

5.3 oz. Biga (see sidebar)

14.1 oz. bread flour

8.8 oz. all-purpose flour, plus more as needed

2 tablespoons extra-virgin olive oil, plus more as needed

1 tablespoon table salt

FOR THE FOCACCIA

2 tablespoons extra-virgin olive oil

⅔ cup water

1 teaspoon table salt

All-purpose flour, as needed

Coarse sea salt, to taste

1   To begin preparations for the dough, warm 50 grams of the water until it is about 105°F. Add the water and the yeast to a bowl and gently stir. Let sit for 5 to 10 minutes. In a large bowl, combine the Biga, flours, yeast, and water. Work the mixture until it just holds together. Transfer the dough to a flour-dusted surface and work it until it is smooth and elastic.

2   Add the olive oil and salt and work the dough until it is developed, elastic, and extensible, about 5 minutes. Form the dough into a ball and place it in an airtight container that is at least three times its size. Let the dough rest for 1 hour at room temperature. After 1 hour, refrigerate the dough in its container for a minimum of 20 hours.

3   Remove the dough from the refrigerator and let it warm to room temperature. Stretch the dough, place it on a flour-dusted baking sheet, and let it sit at room temperature for 2 hours.

4   Place the dough on a flour-dusted work surface and form it into a loose ball, making sure not to compress the core of the dough and deflate it. Grease an 18 × 13–inch baking pan with olive oil, place the dough on the pan, and gently flatten the dough into an oval. Cover with a kitchen towel and let rest at room temperature for 30 minutes to 1 hour.

5   Stretch the dough toward the edges of the baking pan. If the dough does not want to extend to the edges of the pan right away, let it rest for 15 to 20 minutes before trying again. Cover with the kitchen towel and let rest for another 30 minutes to 1 hour.

BIGA

Place 3.5 oz. bread flour, 1.75 oz. water, and ⅛ teaspoon active dry yeast and work the mixture until it is a sticky dough. Coat a mixing bowl with extra-virgin olive oil, place the dough in the bowl, cover it with plastic wrap, and store in a naturally cool place. Let it sit until it has tripled in size, about 18 hours. Use immediately or store in the refrigerator, where it will keep for up to 5 days.

6   To begin preparations for the focaccia, place the oil, water, and table salt in a mixing bowl and stir to combine. Set the mixture aside. Lightly dust the focaccia with flour and press down on the dough with two fingers to make deep indentations. Cover the focaccia with half of the olive oil mixture and let it rest for another 30 minutes.

7   Preheat the oven to 445°F. Cover the focaccia with the remaining olive oil mixture and sprinkle the coarse sea salt over the top. Place in the oven and bake for 15 to 20 minutes, until the focaccia is a light golden brown. As this focaccia is supposed to be soft, it's far better to remove it too early as opposed to too late. Remove and let cool briefly before serving.

PITA BREAD

YIELD: **8 SERVINGS** / ACTIVE TIME: **30 MINUTES** / TOTAL TIME: **1 HOUR**

INGREDIENTS

1 cup lukewarm water (90°F)

1 tablespoon active dry yeast

1 tablespoon sugar

1¾ cups all-purpose flour, plus more as needed

1 cup whole wheat flour

1 tablespoon kosher salt

1   In a large bowl, combine the water, yeast, and sugar. Let the mixture sit for 15 minutes, or until the water is foamy and bubbling. Add the flours and salt and stir until a dough forms. Knead the dough until it is smooth and uniform, about 1 minute. Cover the dough with plastic wrap and set it aside.

2   Preheat the oven to 500°F. Place an upside-down baking sheet on the floor of the oven. Cut the dough into 8 even pieces and roll them into balls. Working with one ball at a time, place it on a flour-dusted surface, press down on the ball to flatten it, and roll out until it is an approximately ¼-inch-thick circle.

3   Place one pita at a time on the baking sheet and bake until it is puffy and starting to brown, about 5 minutes. Remove and serve once all of the pitas have been cooked.

MUSHROOM TOAST
WITH WHIPPED GOAT CHEESE

YIELD: **4 SERVINGS** / ACTIVE TIME: **10 MINUTES** / TOTAL TIME: **45 MINUTES**

INGREDIENTS

½ lb. mushrooms (chestnut recommended), sliced

Extra-virgin olive oil, as needed

Salt, to taste

4 thick slices of sourdough bread

½ cup heavy cream

4 oz. goat cheese, at room temperature

Sunflower seeds, to taste

Chopped fresh rosemary, to taste

Honey, to taste

1 Preheat the oven to 400°F. Place the mushrooms on a baking sheet, drizzle olive oil over them, and season with salt. Place the mushrooms in the oven and roast until they begin to darken, about 10 to 15 minutes. Place the slices of bread on another baking sheet, brush the tops with olive oil, and season with salt. Place the slices of bread in the oven and bake until golden brown, about 10 minutes.

2 While the mushrooms and bread are in the oven, place the cream in a mixing bowl and beat until stiff peaks begin to form. Add the goat cheese and beat until well combined.

3 Remove the mushrooms and bread from the oven and let cool for 5 minutes. Spread the cream-and-goat cheese mixture on the bread and top with the mushrooms. Sprinkle sunflower seeds and rosemary over the goat cheese and drizzle honey over the top.

RUSTICO
WITH HONEY GLAZE

YIELD: **8 SERVINGS** / ACTIVE TIME: **15 MINUTES** / TOTAL TIME: **30 MINUTES**

INGREDIENTS

Canola oil, as needed

4 sheets of frozen puff pastry,
thawed

1 egg white, beaten

½ lb. fresh mozzarella cheese,
sliced

1 cup honey

1 Add canola oil to a Dutch oven until it is 2 inches deep and warm it to 350°F. Cut eight 5-inch circles and eight 4-inch circles from the sheets of puff pastry. Place a slice of cheese in the center of each 5-inch circle. Place a 4-inch circle over the cheese, fold the bottom circle over the edge, and pinch to seal.

2 Place one or two rustico in the oil and fry until the dough is a light golden brown and crispy, about 2 to 3 minutes. Remove from oil and transfer to a paper towel–lined wire rack. Repeat until all eight wraps have been fried. To serve, drizzle some of the honey over the top of each rustico.

PITA CHIPS

YIELD: **8 SERVINGS** / ACTIVE TIME: **10 MINUTES** / TOTAL TIME: **25 MINUTES**

INGREDIENTS

2 pitas, halved
(see page 65 for homemade)

Unsalted butter or extra-virgin
olive oil, as needed

Salt, to taste

Fresh herbs, as needed

1   Preheat the oven to 350°F. Cut each pita half into eighths and place them on a baking sheet, with the inner side facing up.

2   Spread a little bit of butter or olive oil on each piece of pita. Sprinkle salt and any herbs you'd like on top, place in the oven, and bake until the chips are browned and crispy, about 6 minutes. Remove from the oven and let cool before serving.

LAHMACUN SPREAD

Place ¾ lb. ground beef, ½ large onion, chopped, ½ green bell pepper, 1 chopped tomato, 1 bunch of fresh parsley, 1½ teaspoons tahini, 1 tablespoon tomato paste, ¼ teaspoon of red pepper flakes, black pepper, and ground nutmeg, ½ teaspoon of cinnamon, allspice, sumac powder, dried thyme, and table salt, and the juice of 1 lemon wedge in a food processor or blender and puree until the mixture is a smooth paste.

LAHMACUN

YIELD: **1 FLATBREAD** / ACTIVE TIME: **10 MINUTES** / TOTAL TIME: **30 MINUTES**

INGREDIENTS

1 ball of pizza dough

3 tablespoons Lahmacun Spread (see sidebar)

Juice of 1 lemon wedge

Sumac powder, to taste

¼ small red onion, sliced

3 slices of tomato

¼ cucumber, peeled and julienned

1 tablespoon crumbled feta cheese

Extra-virgin olive oil, to taste

Fresh mint leaves, for garnish

1 Preheat the oven to 410°F and place a baking stone or an upside-down baking sheet in the oven as it warms. Place the dough on a piece of parchment paper and gently stretch it into a very thin round. Cover the dough with the Lahmacun Spread.

2 Using a peel or a flat baking sheet, transfer the pizza to the heated baking stone or sheet in the oven. Bake for about 10 minutes, until the crust is golden brown and starting to char. Remove and top with the lemon juice, sumac powder, onion, tomato, cucumber, and feta. Drizzle olive oil over the top and garnish with fresh mint leaves.

ZA'ATAR MANAQISH

YIELD: **1 FLATBREAD** / ACTIVE TIME: **10 MINUTES** / TOTAL TIME: **30 MINUTES**

INGREDIENTS

1 ball of pizza dough

2 tablespoons za'atar seasoning

2 tablespoons extra-virgin olive oil

¼ small red onion, sliced

3 slices of tomato

¼ cucumber, peeled and julienned

2 tablespoons crumbled feta cheese

1 handful of green olives, pitted

1   Preheat the oven to 400°F and place a baking stone or an upside-down baking sheet on the floor of the oven as it warms. Place the dough on a piece of parchment paper and gently stretch it into a very thin round. Spread the za'atar and olive oil over the dough.

2   Using a peel or a flat baking sheet, transfer the pizza to the heated baking stone or sheet in the oven. Bake for about 10 minutes, until the crust is golden brown and starting to char. Remove and top with the onion, tomato, cucumber, feta, and olives.

PARATHA

YIELD: **8 SERVINGS** / ACTIVE TIME: **30 MINUTES** / TOTAL TIME: **1 HOUR**

INGREDIENTS

2 cups pastry flour, plus more
as needed

1 cup whole wheat flour

¼ teaspoon kosher salt

1 cup warm water (110°F)

5 tablespoons extra-virgin olive
oil, plus more as needed

5 tablespoons ghee or melted
unsalted butter

1   Place the flours and salt in the work bowl of a stand mixer fitted with the paddle attachment. Turn on low and slowly add the warm water. Mix until incorporated and then slowly add the olive oil. When the oil has been incorporated, place the dough on a flour-dusted work surface and knead until it is quite smooth, about 8 minutes.

2   Divide the dough into 8 small balls and dust them with flour. Use your hands to roll each ball into a long rope, and then coil each rope into a large disk. Use a rolling pin to flatten the disks until they are no more than ¼ inch thick. Lightly brush each disk with a small amount of olive oil.

3   Place a cast-iron skillet over very high heat for about 4 minutes. Brush the pan with some of the ghee or melted butter and place a disk of the dough on the pan. Cook until it is blistered and brown, about 1 minute. Turn over and cook the other side. Transfer the cooked paratha to a plate and repeat with the remaining disks. Serve warm or at room temperature.

NOTE: If you want to freeze any extras, make sure to place parchment paper between them to prevent them from melding together in the freezer.

MUFFULETTA

YIELD: **4 TO 6 SERVINGS** / ACTIVE TIME: **45 MINUTES** / TOTAL TIME: **24 HOURS**

INGREDIENTS

1 red bell pepper

1 cup sun-dried tomatoes in olive
oil, drained and chopped

1 cup pitted green olives,
chopped

1 cup pitted black olives, chopped

¼ cup extra-virgin olive oil

¼ cup chopped fresh parsley

2 tablespoons fresh lemon juice

1 teaspoon dried oregano

1 loaf of Italian or French bread,
halved lengthwise

2 cups lettuce, torn

4 oz. mortadella, sliced thin

4 oz. provolone cheese,
sliced thin

4 oz. soppressata, sliced thin

1   Preheat the oven to 400°F. Place the bell pepper on a baking sheet, place it in the oven, and roast, turning it occasionally, until it is charred all over, about 25 minutes. Remove from the oven and let cool. When cool enough to handle, remove the charred flesh, chop the pepper, and discard the seeds and stem. Place the roasted pepper in a mixing bowl.

2   Add the tomatoes, olives, oil, parsley, lemon juice, and oregano to the bowl. Cover and refrigerate overnight.

3   Drain the olive mixture and reserve the liquid. Remove most of the crumb from one of the halves of the bread and generously brush the cut sides with the reserved liquid. Fill the piece of bread with the crumb removed with half of the olive mixture and top with half of the lettuce and all of the mortadella, provolone, and soppressata. Layer the remaining lettuce over the soppressata and top with the remaining olive mixture and the other piece of bread. Wrap the sandwich in plastic wrap and place it on a large plate. Place another plate on top and weight it down with a good-sized cookbook or something similar. Refrigerate for at least 1 hour before slicing into the desired amount of servings.

ROSEMARY CRACKERS

YIELD: **6 CRACKERS** / ACTIVE TIME: **15 MINUTES** / TOTAL TIME: **1 HOUR AND 10 MINUTES**

INGREDIENTS

⅛ teaspoon active dry yeast

1 tablespoon lukewarm water (90°F)

½ cup all-purpose flour, plus more as needed

1 teaspoon kosher salt

Pinch of sugar

2 tablespoons finely chopped fresh rosemary

Extra-virgin olive oil, as needed

1   Preheat the oven to 350°F. Place the yeast and the water in a mixing bowl, stir gently, and let stand for 10 minutes.

2   Add the remaining ingredients, except for the olive oil, to the bowl and knead the mixture until it is a smooth dough.

3   Cover the bowl with a kitchen towel and let it stand in a naturally warm spot until the dough doubles in size, about 20 minutes.

4   Place the dough on a flour-dusted work surface and roll it out as thin as you can without it tearing.

5   Cut the dough into the desired shapes and place them on a parchment-lined baking sheet. Brush the top of each cracker with a small amount of olive oil.

6   Place the crackers in the oven and bake for 20 minutes, or until golden brown. Remove and let the crackers cool on a wire rack before serving.

NOTE: Any herb, sesame seeds, or chopped dried fruit can be substituted for the rosemary here, so don't be afraid to experiment.

CROSTINI

YIELD: **6 SERVINGS** / ACTIVE TIME: **15 MINUTES** / TOTAL TIME: **30 MINUTES**

INGREDIENTS

1 baguette, sliced

2 tablespoons extra-virgin olive oil, plus more to taste

Salt and pepper, to taste

1   Preheat the oven to 400°F. Brush the slices of baguette with the olive oil and place them on a baking sheet. Place in the oven and bake for 12 to 15 minutes, turning the slices over halfway through. When the slices are golden brown on both sides, remove from the oven.

2   Top the crostini as desired, drizzle olive oil over them, and season with salt and pepper.

NOTE: There are limitless ways you can utilize these crostini. Those pictured feature ricotta and pea shoots, but you can top them with anything you like, or just serve them on the side and let people top them as they please with a number of the other preparations in this book.

CHEESE TWISTS

YIELD: **12 SERVINGS** / ACTIVE TIME: **15 MINUTES** / TOTAL TIME: **30 MINUTES**

INGREDIENTS

2 sheets of frozen puff pastry, thawed

All-purpose flour, as needed

½ cup grated Fontina cheese

½ cup grated Parmesan cheese

1 teaspoon finely chopped fresh thyme

1 teaspoon black pepper

1 egg, beaten

1   Preheat the oven to 375°F and line a baking sheet with parchment paper. Place the sheets of puff pastry on a flour-dusted surface and roll out until the sheets are approximately 10 x 12–inch rectangles.

2   Place the cheeses, thyme, and pepper in a mixing bowl and stir to combine.

3   Lightly brush the tops of the pastry sheets with the egg. Sprinkle the cheese mixture over them and gently press down so it adheres to the pastry. Cut the sheets into ¼-inch-wide strips and twist them.

4   Place the twists on the baking sheet, place in the oven, and bake for 12 to 15 minutes, until twists are golden brown and puffy. Turn the twists over and bake for another 2 to 3 minutes. Remove from the oven and let the twists cool on a wire rack before serving.

Goat Cheese with Herbs, page 105

DUMPLINGS & OTHER DECADENT BITES

Much debate rages over what is and isn't a dumpling, but almost no one is out there arguing that they aren't delicious. The joy that these small pockets and nibbles provide is considerable, particularly when partnered with the sauces and dips that appear earlier in this book.

If a dumpling isn't going to hit the mark one particular evening, there are a dozen or so off-the-beaten-path preparations that will put a smile on everyone's face.

HUSH PUPPIES

YIELD: **8 SERVINGS** / ACTIVE TIME: **15 MINUTES** / TOTAL TIME: **1 HOUR AND 15 MINUTES**

INGREDIENTS

1 cup all-purpose flour

1½ cups cornmeal

2 tablespoons baking powder

2 tablespoons sugar

1 tablespoon baking soda

2 teaspoons kosher salt

½ teaspoon cayenne pepper

1¼ cups buttermilk

2 eggs

1 large yellow onion, grated

Canola oil, as needed

1   Place the flour, cornmeal, baking powder, sugar, baking soda, salt, and cayenne in a large bowl and stir to combine.

2   Place the buttermilk, eggs, and the grated onion (along with any juices that have collected) in a bowl and stir to combine. Add the wet mixture to the dry mixture, stir to combine, and let the batter stand for 1 hour.

3   Add canola oil to a large Dutch oven until it is 2 inches deep and warm over medium heat until it is 350°F. Drop tablespoons of the batter into the oil, while making sure to not crowd the Dutch oven. Cook, turning the hush puppies as they brown, until they are crispy and golden brown, about 3 to 4 minutes. Transfer the cooked hush puppies to a paper towel–lined plate to drain and let them cool briefly before serving.

PAPAS RELLENAS

YIELD: **4 SERVINGS** / ACTIVE TIME: **30 MINUTES** / TOTAL TIME: **1 HOUR**

INGREDIENTS

3 lbs. potatoes, peeled and chopped

1 garlic clove, minced

2 teaspoons kosher salt

1 teaspoon black pepper

1 tablespoon extra-virgin olive oil

1 small green bell pepper, stemmed, seeded, and minced

1 yellow onion, minced

½ lb. ground beef

2 tablespoons tomato paste

¼ cup pitted and sliced green olives

¼ cup raisins

½ teaspoon paprika

Canola oil, as needed

2 eggs, lightly beaten

½ cup bread crumbs

1 Bring water to a boil in a large saucepan. Add the potatoes, cover the pan, and cook until the potatoes are fork-tender, about 20 minutes. Drain the potatoes, place them in a large bowl, and mash until smooth. Add the garlic and half of the salt and pepper and stir to incorporate.

2 Warm the olive oil in a skillet over medium heat. When the oil starts to shimmer, add the bell pepper and onion and cook, stirring frequently, until the onion is translucent, about 3 minutes. Add the ground beef and cook, breaking it up with a fork, until it is browned, about 10 minutes. Stir in the tomato paste, olives, raisins, paprika, and the remaining salt and pepper and cook for 2 minutes. Transfer the mixture to a paper towel–lined baking sheet and let it drain.

3 Add canola oil to a Dutch oven until it is 2 inches deep and bring it to 375°F. Place the eggs and bread crumbs in two separate bowls. Place 2 tablespoons of the potato mixture in one hand, pat it down until it is flat, and then place a tablespoon of the ground beef mixture in the center. Shape the potato around the filling to create a ball and dip the ball into the egg. Roll the ball in the bread crumbs until coated and place on a parchment-lined baking sheet. Repeat until all of the potato mixture and ground beef mixture have been used up.

4 Working in batches, place the balls in the hot oil and deep-fry until golden brown, about 2 minutes. Remove with a slotted spoon and set them on a paper towel–lined plate to drain and cool slightly before serving.

EMPANADAS

YIELD: **4 SERVINGS** / ACTIVE TIME: **30 MINUTES** / TOTAL TIME: **1 HOUR AND 45 MINUTES**

INGREDIENTS

FOR THE DOUGH

¼ teaspoon kosher salt

6 tablespoons warm water (110°F)

1½ cups all-purpose flour, plus more as needed

3 tablespoons lard or unsalted butter, cut into small pieces

FOR THE FILLING

2 teaspoons extra-virgin olive oil

1 yellow onion, minced

1 garlic clove, minced

¾ lb. ground pork

1 (14 oz.) can of crushed tomatoes, drained

½ teaspoon kosher salt

¼ teaspoon black pepper

1 cinnamon stick

2 whole cloves

2 tablespoons raisins

2 teaspoons apple cider vinegar

2 tablespoons slivered almonds, toasted

Canola oil, as needed

1 To prepare the dough, dissolve the salt in the warm water. Place the flour in a mixing bowl, add the lard or butter, and work the mixture with a pastry blender until it is coarse crumbs. Add the salted water and knead the mixture until a stiff dough forms. Cut the dough into eight pieces, cover them with plastic wrap, and chill in the refrigerator for 20 minutes.

2 To prepare the filling, place the olive oil in a skillet and warm over medium heat. When the oil starts to shimmer, add the onion and cook until it has softened, about 5 minutes. Add the garlic, cook for 2 minutes, and then add the ground pork. Cook, while breaking it up with a fork, until light brown, about 5 minutes. Drain off any fat and stir in the tomatoes, salt, pepper, cinnamon stick, cloves, raisins, and vinegar. Simmer until the mixture is thick, about 30 minutes. Remove the pan from heat, remove the cloves and cinnamon stick, and discard them. Let the mixture cool and then fold in the toasted almonds.

3 Add canola oil to a Dutch oven until it is 2 inches deep and warm to 350°F over medium heat. Preheat the oven to 200°F and place a platter in the oven. Place the pieces of dough on a flour-dusted work surface and roll each one into a 5-inch circle. Place 3 tablespoons of the filling in the center of one circle, brush the edge with water, and fold into a half-moon. Pinch the edge to seal the empanada tight while gently pressing down to remove as much air as possible. Repeat with the remaining filling and pieces of dough.

4 Working in two batches, place the empanadas in the hot oil and fry until golden brown, about 5 minutes. Drain the cooked empanadas on paper towels and place them in the warm oven while you cook the next batch.

PUNJABI SAMOSA

YIELD: **16 SAMOSA** / ACTIVE TIME: **45 MINUTES** / TOTAL TIME: **1 HOUR AND 30 MINUTES**

1   To begin preparations for the wrappers, place the flour and salt in a mixing bowl and use your hands to combine. Add the oil and work the mixture with your hands until it is a coarse meal. Add the water and knead the mixture until a smooth, firm dough forms. If the dough is too dry, incorporate more water, adding 1 tablespoon at a time. Cover the bowl with a kitchen towel and set aside.

2   To begin preparations for the filling, place the potatoes in a saucepan and cover with water. Bring the water to a boil and cook until fork-tender, about 20 minutes. Transfer to a bowl, mash until smooth, and set aside.

3   Place the olive oil in a skillet and warm over medium heat. Add the crushed seeds and toast until fragrant, about 2 minutes, shaking the pan frequently. Add the ginger, garlic, and jalapeño, stir-fry for 2 minutes, and then add the chili powder, turmeric, amchoor powder, and garam masala. Cook for another minute before adding the mashed potatoes. Stir to combine, season with salt, and taste the mixture. Adjust the seasoning as necessary, transfer the mixture to a bowl, and let it cool completely.

4   Divide the dough for the wrappers into eight pieces and roll each one out into a 6-inch circle on a flour-dusted work surface. Cut the circles in half and brush the flat edge of each piece with water. Fold one corner of the flat edge toward the other to make a cone and pinch to seal. Fill each cone one-third of the way with the filling, brush the opening with water, and pinch to seal. Place the sealed samosas on a parchment-lined baking sheet.

5   Add canola oil to a Dutch oven until it is 2 inches deep and warm to 325°F over medium heat. Working in batches, add the filled samosas to the hot oil and fry, turning them as they cook, until they are golden brown, about 5 minutes. Transfer the cooked samosas to a paper towel–lined plate and serve once they have all been cooked.

INGREDIENTS

FOR THE WRAPPERS

2 cups maida flour, plus more
as needed

¼ teaspoon kosher salt

2 tablespoons extra-virgin
olive oil

½ cup water, plus more as needed

FOR THE FILLING

2 russet potatoes, peeled
and chopped

2 tablespoons extra-virgin
olive oil

1 teaspoon coriander seeds, crushed

½ teaspoon fennel seeds, crushed

Pinch of fenugreek seeds, crushed

1-inch piece of fresh ginger, peeled
and grated

1 garlic clove, grated

1 teaspoon minced jalapeño pepper

2 teaspoons chili powder

¾ teaspoon turmeric

1 tablespoon amchoor powder

½ teaspoon garam masala

Salt, to taste

Canola oil, as needed

INGREDIENTS

FOR THE DOUGH

3 cups all-purpose flour, plus more as needed

¾ teaspoon kosher salt

½ cup lard or unsalted butter, cut into small pieces

1 large egg, beaten

¼ cup cold water, plus more as needed

2 teaspoons distilled white vinegar

FOR THE FILLING

¾ lb. skirt steak, cut into ½-inch cubes

¼ cup peeled and chopped parsnips

¼ cup peeled and chopped turnips

1 small onion, chopped

1 cup peeled and chopped potato

1 tablespoon chopped fresh thyme

2 tablespoons tomato paste

Salt and pepper, to taste

1 large egg, beaten

1 tablespoon water

CORNISH PASTIES

YIELD: **6 SERVINGS** / ACTIVE TIME: **30 MINUTES** / TOTAL TIME: **1 HOUR AND 15 MINUTES**

1   To prepare the dough, place the flour and salt in a bowl, add the lard or butter, and use a pastry blender to work the mixture until it is coarse crumbs. Beat the egg, water, and vinegar together in a separate bowl and then drizzle this over the flour mixture. Use the pastry blender to work the mixture until it starts to hold together. Knead the dough with your hands, adding water in 1-teaspoon increments if it is too dry. Cut the dough into 6 pieces, cover them with plastic wrap, and chill in the refrigerator.

2   Preheat the oven to 400°F and prepare the filling. Place all of the ingredients, except for the egg and water, in a bowl and stir to combine. Place the egg and water in a separate bowl and beat to combine.

3   Place the pieces of dough on a flour-dusted work surface, roll each one into an 8-inch circle, and place ½ cup of the filling in the center of each circle. Brush the edge of each circle with water, fold into a half-moon, and crimp the edge to seal, gently pressing down to remove as much air as possible. Place the sealed handpies on a parchment-lined baking sheet.

4   Brush the handpies with the egg wash and use a paring knife to make a small incision in the side of each one. Bake in the oven for 15 minutes, reduce the temperature to 350°F, and bake for another 25 minutes. Remove from the oven and let cool on a wire rack before serving.

ASPARAGUS TART

YIELD: **8 SERVINGS** / ACTIVE TIME: **15 MINUTES** / TOTAL TIME: **45 MINUTES**

INGREDIENTS

½ teaspoon kosher salt, plus
more to taste

1 lb. asparagus, trimmed

1½ cups ricotta cheese

¼ cup extra-virgin olive oil

2 tablespoons heavy cream

2 egg yolks

1 teaspoon chopped fresh
rosemary

1 Savory Tart Shell (see page 57)

1   Preheat the oven to 350°F. Bring a pot of water to a boil. Add salt until the water tastes just shy of seawater, add the asparagus, and cook for 2 minutes. Drain, pat dry, and set aside.

2   Place all of the remaining ingredients, aside from the tart shell, in a mixing bowl and stir to combine. Distribute the mixture evenly in the tart shell, arrange the asparagus in the custard, and place the tart in the oven. Bake until the custard is set and golden brown, about 25 minutes. Remove from the oven and serve warm or at room temperature.

NOTE: This simple custard and the recipe for the tart shell come courtesy of the Tamar Adler's magnificent book, *An Everlasting Meal*. The pair is so reliable and versatile that any vegetable can comfortably be swapped in for the asparagus.

CHICKPEA POUTINE

YIELD: **4 SERVINGS** / ACTIVE TIME: **45 MINUTES** / TOTAL TIME: **2 HOURS**

INGREDIENTS

1 cup chickpea flour

2 teaspoons kosher salt

1 teaspoon garlic powder

2 tablespoons dried parsley

Pinch of cumin

2 cups boiling water

Canola oil, as needed

½ lb. leftover braised short rib

½ cup crumbled feta cheese

1 Place the flour, salt, garlic powder, parsley, and cumin in a mixing bowl and stir to combine. Add the boiling water and beat until the batter is smooth. Pour the batter into a small baking dish (small enough that the batter is about 1 inch deep), cover with plastic wrap, and refrigerate for 1 hour.

2 Turn the mixture out onto a cutting board and cut it into wide strips.

3 Add canola oil to a Dutch oven until it is about 3 inches deep and warm it to 350°F over medium heat. Add the chickpea fries and turn the fries as they cook until they are crispy and golden brown, 3 to 4 minutes. Place on a paper towel–lined plate to drain.

4 Place the short rib in a small saucepan, add about ½ cup of water, and bring it to a simmer. Cook until the liquid has reduced by half.

5 Arrange the fries on a platter and spoon the gravy from the short rib over them. Top with the short rib, sprinkle the feta over the fries, and serve.

CHEESY POOFS

YIELD: **4 SERVINGS** / ACTIVE TIME: **15 MINUTES** / TOTAL TIME: **35 MINUTES**

INGREDIENTS

Canola oil, as needed

2 cups Smoked Sweet Potato Puree (see page 44)

1 egg

½ cup all-purpose flour

½ teaspoon baking powder

¼ cup grated Asiago cheese

¼ cup grated Parmesan cheese

⅓ cup shredded mozzarella cheese

1 Add canola oil to a Dutch oven until it is 3 inches deep and warm to 350°F over medium heat. Place the puree and egg in a mixing bowl. Add the flour and baking powder and stir until the mixture is smooth.

2 Add the cheeses one at a time and fold to incorporate. Form tablespoons of the mixture into balls and gently place them in the oil. Turn the balls as they cook until they are golden brown, 3 to 4 minutes. Remove and drain on a paper towel–lined plate before serving.

GOAT CHEESE WITH HERBS

YIELD: **4 SERVINGS** / ACTIVE TIME: **10 MINUTES** / TOTAL TIME: **1 HOUR AND 10 MINUTES**

INGREDIENTS

½ lb. goat cheese

2 tablespoons chopped
fresh tarragon

2 tablespoons chopped
fresh chives

2 tablespoons chopped
fresh thyme

1 cup extra-virgin olive oil

2 garlic cloves, chopped

1 teaspoon kosher salt

1   Slice the goat cheese into rounds. Gently roll the rounds in the herbs and gently press down so that the herbs adhere to the surface of the cheese.

2   Layer the rounds in a mason jar. Pour the olive oil over them until they are covered. Add the garlic and salt and let the mixture sit for an hour before serving. The goat cheese will keep in the refrigerator for up to 3 months.

GRILLED HALLOUMI CHEESE

YIELD: **8 SERVINGS** / ACTIVE TIME: **10 MINUTES** / TOTAL TIME: **10 MINUTES**

INGREDIENTS

½ lb. Halloumi cheese, cut into 8 pieces

Extra-virgin olive oil, as needed

1   Warm a cast-iron grill pan over medium heat. Place the cheese in a small bowl, drizzle olive oil over it, and toss to coat.

2   Place the cheese in the pan and cook until charred on both sides, about 2 minutes per side.

FALAFEL

YIELD: **6 SERVINGS** / ACTIVE TIME: **30 MINUTES** / TOTAL TIME: **1 HOUR**

INGREDIENTS

1½ (14 oz.) cans of chickpeas, drained and rinsed

1 small onion, grated

3 garlic cloves

¼ cup all-purpose flour

2 tablespoons chopped fresh parsley

1 tablespoon fresh lemon juice

1 tablespoon coriander

2 teaspoons cumin

1 teaspoon baking soda

Salt and cayenne pepper, to taste

Canola oil, as needed

1   Place the chickpeas in a food processor. Add the remaining ingredients, except for the canola oil, and blitz until the mixture is a smooth paste, scraping the work bowl as necessary.

2   Form the mixture into 1-inch balls, place them on a parchment-lined baking sheet, cover tightly with plastic wrap, and refrigerate for 20 minutes.

3   Add canola oil to a Dutch oven until it is approximately 2 inches deep and warm to 375°F over medium-high heat. Working in batches, add the falafel and fry until browned all over, about 3 minutes. Transfer the cooked falafel to a paper towel–lined plate to drain and serve once all of them have been cooked.

SMOKY & SPICY ALMONDS

YIELD: **2 CUPS** / ACTIVE TIME: **10 MINUTES** / TOTAL TIME: **45 MINUTES**

INGREDIENTS

4 tablespoons unsalted
butter, melted

4 teaspoons
Worcestershire sauce

1 teaspoon cumin

2 teaspoons chili powder

1 teaspoon garlic powder

½ teaspoon onion powder

1 teaspoon cayenne pepper

1 teaspoon kosher salt

2 cups whole almonds

1   Preheat the oven to 350°F and line a baking sheet with parchment paper. Place all of the ingredients, except for the almonds, in a mixing bowl and stir until combined. Add the almonds and toss to coat.

2   Transfer the almonds to the baking sheet, place it in the oven, and roast for about 15 minutes, until the almonds are fragrant and a darker brown. Turn the almonds occasionally as they roast. Remove and let cool before serving.

BAKED APPLES

YIELD: **6 SERVINGS** / ACTIVE TIME: **15 MINUTES** / TOTAL TIME: **1 HOUR**

INGREDIENTS

6 apples

3 tablespoons unsalted butter, melted

6 tablespoons blackberry jam

2 oz. goat cheese, cut into 6 rounds

1 Preheat the oven to 350°F. Slice the tops off of the apples and set aside. Use a paring knife to cut a circle around the apples' cores and then scoop out their centers. Make sure to leave a ½-inch-thick wall inside each apple.

2 Rub the inside and outside of the apples with some of the melted butter. Place the jam and goat cheese in a mixing bowl and stir to combine. Fill the apples' cavities with the mixture, place the tops back on the apples, and set them aside.

3 Grease a baking dish with the remaining butter, place the apples in the dish, and place the dish in the oven. Bake until the apples are tender, 25 to 30 minutes. Remove from the oven and let cool briefly before serving.

SOUTHERN DEVILED EGGS

YIELD: **6 EGGS** / ACTIVE TIME: **15 MINUTES** / TOTAL TIME: **30 MINUTES**

INGREDIENTS

6 hard-boiled eggs

2 tablespoons yellow mustard

2 tablespoons mayonnaise

2 teaspoons whole-grain mustard

2 cornichons, diced

2 teaspoons diced pimento pepper

Salt and pepper, to taste

Fresh parsley, chopped, for garnish

Fresh dill, chopped, for garnish

1 slice of Spam, cut into triangles and fried, for garnish (optional)

1   Cut the eggs in half, remove the yolks, and place them in a small bowl. Add all of the remaining ingredients, except for the garnishes, and stir until thoroughly combined.

2   Spoon the yolk mixture into the cavities in the egg whites. Garnish with parsley, dill, and, if desired, the Spam.

BAKED BRIE, TWO WAYS

YIELD: **6 SERVINGS** / ACTIVE TIME: **10 MINUTES** / TOTAL TIME: **25 MINUTES**

INGREDIENTS

½ lb. wheel of Brie cheese

FOR THE SAVORY TOPPING

¼ cup chopped roasted tomatoes

¼ cup chopped artichoke hearts

2 tablespoons chopped olives

1 tablespoon capers

Pinch of black pepper

FOR THE SWEET TOPPING

¼ cup chopped pecans

¼ cup chopped dried apricots

⅓ cup Divina fig spread

¼ cup dried cherries

Pinch of cinnamon

1   Preheat the oven to 350°F. Place the cheese in a ceramic dish. Combine the ingredients for your chosen mixture in a mixing bowl and top the Brie with it.

2   Place in the oven and bake for 15 minutes, until the cheese is gooey.

3   Remove from the oven and serve with crackers or toasted bread.

CASHEL BLUE FRITTERS

YIELD: **12 FRITTERS** / ACTIVE TIME: **25 MINUTES** / TOTAL TIME: **40 MINUTES**

INGREDIENTS

Canola oil, as needed

3 eggs

¼ cup all-purpose flour

1 cup panko, finely ground

6 oz. Cashel blue cheese, cut into 12 cubes

1   Add oil to a Dutch oven until it is 2 inches deep and warm it to 350°F over medium heat. Place the eggs in a bowl and beat them with a fork. Place the flour and panko in separate bowls. Dredge the cheese in the flour and shake to remove any excess. Dredge the cheese in the egg wash until evenly coated. Remove from the egg wash, shake to remove any excess, and dredge in the panko until coated.

2   Place the breaded cheese in the hot oil and fry until golden brown, 3 to 4 minutes. Use a slotted spoon to remove the fritters from the oil, set on paper towels to drain, and season with salt. Let the fritters cool slightly before serving.

NOTE: You can strain and reuse the oil once it has cooled.

VEGETABLE STOCK

Place 2 tablespoons extra-virgin olive oil, 2 trimmed and well rinsed leeks, 2 peeled and sliced carrots, 2 celery stalks, 2 sliced onions, and 3 unpeeled, smashed garlic cloves in a large stockpot and cook over low heat until the liquid the vegetables release has evaporated. Add 2 sprigs of fresh parsley and thyme, 1 bay leaf, 8 cups water, ½ teaspoon black peppercorns, and salt to taste. Raise the heat to high and bring the stock to a boil. Reduce heat so that the stock simmers and cook for 2 hours, skimming to remove any impurities that float to the surface. Strain the stock through a fine sieve, let the stock cool slightly, and place it in the refrigerator, uncovered, to chill. Remove the fat layer and cover. The stock will keep in the refrigerator for 3 to 5 days, and in the freezer for up to 3 months.

POLENTA FRIES

YIELD: **4 SERVINGS** / ACTIVE TIME: **30 MINUTES** / TOTAL TIME: **2 HOURS AND 30 MINUTES**

INGREDIENTS

2½ cups milk

2½ cups Vegetable Stock (see sidebar)

2 cups medium-grain cornmeal

2 tablespoons unsalted butter

1 teaspoon kosher salt, plus more to taste

½ teaspoon black pepper

½ teaspoon dried oregano

½ teaspoon dried thyme

½ teaspoon dried rosemary

Canola oil, as needed

¼ cup grated Parmesan cheese, for garnish

2 tablespoons finely chopped fresh rosemary, for garnish

1 Coat a large, rimmed baking sheet with nonstick cooking spray. Place the milk and stock in a saucepan and bring to a boil. Whisk in the cornmeal, reduce heat to low and cook, while stirring constantly, until all of the liquid has been absorbed and the polenta is creamy, about 30 minutes.

2 Stir in the butter, salt, pepper, oregano, thyme, and dried rosemary. When they have been incorporated, transfer the polenta to the greased baking sheet and even out the surface with a rubber spatula. Refrigerate for 2 hours.

3 Carefully invert the baking sheet over a cutting board so that the polenta falls onto it. Slice the polenta in half lengthwise and cut each piece into 4-inch-long and 1-inch-wide strips.

4 Add canola oil to a Dutch oven until it is 2 inches deep and warm it to 375°F over medium heat. Working in batches of two, place the strips in the oil and fry, turning them as they cook, until golden brown, 2 to 4 minutes. Transfer the cooked fries to a paper towel–lined plate to drain. When all of the fries have been cooked, sprinkle the Parmesan and fresh rosemary over them and serve.

ARANCINI

YIELD: **8 SERVINGS** / ACTIVE TIME: **30 MINUTES** / TOTAL TIME: **1 HOUR AND 30 MINUTES**

INGREDIENTS

5 cups Chicken Stock
(see sidebar)

1 stick of unsalted butter

2 cups Arborio rice

1 small white onion, grated

1 cup white wine

4 oz. Fontina cheese, grated

Salt and pepper, to taste

Canola oil, as needed

6 large eggs, beaten

5 cups panko

1   Bring the stock to a simmer in a large saucepan. In a skillet, melt the butter over high heat. Once the butter is foaming, add the rice and onion and cook until the rice has a toasty fragrance, about 4 minutes. Deglaze the skillet with the white wine and cook until the wine has almost completely been absorbed. Then, reduce the heat to medium-high and begin adding the stock ¼ cup at a time, stirring until it has been incorporated. Continue this process until the rice is al dente.

2   Turn off the heat, stir in the cheese, and season with salt and pepper. Pour the mixture onto a rimmed baking sheet and let it cool.

3   Add the oil to a Dutch oven until it is 2 inches deep and warm over medium heat until it reaches 350°F. When the rice mixture is cool, form it into golf ball–sized spheres. Dip them into in the eggs and then dip into the panko until coated all over. Place the balls in the oil and cook until warmed through and golden brown, 3 to 4 minutes. Transfer to a paper towel–lined plate and let them cool before serving.

CHICKEN STOCK

Place 3 lbs. rinsed chicken bones in a large stockpot, cover them with water, and bring to a boil. Add 1 chopped onion, 2 chopped carrots, 3 chopped celery stalks, 3 unpeeled, smashed garlic cloves, 3 sprigs of fresh thyme, 1 teaspoon black peppercorns, 1 bay leaf, and salt to taste and reduce the heat so that the stock simmers. Cook for 2 hours, skimming to remove any impurities that float to the surface. Strain the stock through a fine sieve, let the stock cool slightly, and place it in the refrigerator, uncovered, to chill. Remove the fat layer and cover. The stock will keep in the refrigerator for 3 to 5 days, and in the freezer for up to 3 months.

IN THE GARDEN

Stuffed Mushrooms, page 151

Thankfully, we've all started to realize that vegetables are so much more than salad, and have the ability to serve as the centerpiece of a meal. They also have the ability to star in a supporting role.

This chapter gathers recipes intended to meet these charges, providing a collection of dishes that will bring balance to your table, and celebrate the incredible array of flavors made available by Mother Nature.

TABBOULEH

YIELD: **4 CUPS** / ACTIVE TIME: **15 MINUTES** / TOTAL TIME: **45 MINUTES**

INGREDIENTS

½ cup bulgur wheat

1½ cups boiling water

½ teaspoon kosher salt,
plus more to taste

½ cup fresh lemon juice

2 cups fresh parsley, chopped

2 cucumbers peeled, seeded,
and diced

2 tomatoes, seeded and diced

6 scallions, trimmed and sliced

1 cup fresh mint leaves, chopped

2 tablespoons extra-virgin
olive oil

Black pepper, to taste

½ cup crumbled feta cheese

1   Place the bulgur in a heatproof bowl and add the boiling water, salt, and half of the lemon juice. Cover and let sit for about 20 minutes, until the bulgur has absorbed all of the liquid and is tender. Drain any excess liquid if necessary. Let the bulgur cool completely.

2   When the bulgur has cooled, add the parsley, cucumber, tomato, scallions, mint, olive oil, black pepper, and remaining lemon juice. Top with the feta and serve.

WATERMELON & FETA SALAD

YIELD: **4 SERVINGS** / ACTIVE TIME: **10 MINUTES** / TOTAL TIME: **15 MINUTES**

INGREDIENTS

FOR THE SALAD

Flesh of ½ watermelon, cubed

1 cucumber, diced

15 fresh mint leaves, torn

15 fresh basil leaves, torn

½ cup crumbled feta cheese

FOR THE VINAIGRETTE

2 tablespoons honey

2 tablespoons fresh lemon juice

1 tablespoon extra-virgin olive oil

Salt, to taste

1   To begin preparations for the salad, place all of the ingredients, except for the feta, in a salad bowl and toss to combine.

2   To prepare the vinaigrette, place all of the ingredients in a mixing bowl and whisk vigorously until combined.

3   Add the vinaigrette to the salad, gently toss to combine, and top with the feta.

EGGPLANT RINGS

YIELD: **4 SERVINGS** / ACTIVE TIME: **40 MINUTES** / TOTAL TIME: **1 HOUR**

INGREDIENTS

1 large eggplant, trimmed and
sliced

2 eggs, beaten

1 cup all-purpose flour

1 cup panko

1 tablespoon kosher salt

1 tablespoon black pepper

Canola oil, as needed

¼ cup red zhug

¼ cup ketchup

1   Cut the centers out of the slices of eggplant, creating
rings that have an about an inch of eggplant inside.

2   Place the eggs, flour, and panko in separate bowls. Add
the salt and pepper to the bowl of panko and stir to
combine. Dip an eggplant ring into the flour, then the
egg, followed by the panko, until the ring is entirely
coated. Place the coated rings on a parchment-lined
baking sheet.

3   Add canola oil to a cast-iron skillet until it is about 1
inch deep and warm to 375°F over medium-high heat.
Working in batches of 4 or 5 rings at a time, gently lay
them in the oil and cook until browned and crispy all
over, about 4 minutes, turning as necessary. Place the
cooked rings on a paper towel–lined plate to drain.

4   Place the zhug and ketchup in a small bowl, stir to
combine, and serve alongside the eggplant rings.

PEPPERS STUFFED WITH GREEK SALAD

YIELD: **4 SERVINGS** / ACTIVE TIME: **10 MINUTES** / TOTAL TIME: **25 MINUTES**

INGREDIENTS

4 yellow bell peppers, seeded
and halved

12 cherry tomatoes, halved

2 garlic cloves, minced

2 tablespoons extra-virgin
olive oil

½ cup crumbled feta cheese

1 cup black olives, pitted

Salt and pepper, to taste

Leaves from 1 bunch of
fresh basil

1   Preheat the oven to 375°F and place the peppers on a parchment-lined baking sheet.

2   Place the cherry tomatoes, garlic, olive oil, feta, and black olives in a mixing bowl and stir to combine. Divide the mixture between the peppers, place them in the oven, and roast until the peppers start to collapse, 10 to 15 minutes.

3   Remove the peppers from the oven and let cool slightly. Season with salt and pepper and top with the basil leaves before serving.

INGREDIENTS

FOR THE SALAD

1 pint of cherry tomatoes

1 tablespoon extra-virgin olive oil

5 garlic cloves, crushed

Leaves from 2 sprigs of
fresh thyme

½ teaspoon kosher salt, plus
more to taste

¼ teaspoon black pepper, plus
more to taste

3 zucchini, sliced thin with a
mandoline

2 summer squash, sliced thin
with a mandoline

1 red bell pepper, stemmed,
seeded, and sliced thin with a
mandoline

FOR THE VINAIGRETTE

1 tablespoon sliced fresh chives

1 teaspoon chopped fresh thyme

1 teaspoon dried oregano

1 tablespoon chopped
fresh parsley

3 tablespoons apple cider vinegar

1 tablespoon honey

2 teaspoons diced shallot

1 teaspoon kosher salt

¼ teaspoon black pepper

¼ cup extra-virgin olive oil

SHAVED SQUASH SALAD
WITH HERB VINAIGRETTE

YIELD: **6 SERVINGS** / ACTIVE TIME: **15 MINUTES** / TOTAL TIME: **1 HOUR**

1 To begin preparations for the salad, set the oven's broiler to high. Place the cherry tomatoes, olive oil, garlic, thyme, salt, and black pepper in a mixing bowl and toss until the tomatoes are evenly coated. Place the tomatoes on a baking sheet, place in the oven, and broil until their skins begin to burst, 6 to 8 minutes. Remove from the oven and let cool completely.

2 To prepare the vinaigrette, place all of the ingredients, except for the olive oil, in a mixing bowl and whisk to combine. Add the oil in a slow stream while whisking to incorporate. Season to taste and set aside.

3 Place the zucchini, squash, and bell pepper in a large mixing bowl, season with salt and pepper, and add the vinaigrette. Toss to evenly coat, plate the salad, and sprinkle the blistered tomatoes over the top.

BUTTERMILK CHARRED BRASSICAS

YIELD: **4 SERVINGS** / ACTIVE TIME: **20 MINUTES** / TOTAL TIME: **45 MINUTES**

INGREDIENTS

1 teaspoon kosher salt, plus more
to taste

1 small head of cauliflower, cut
into bite-sized pieces

1 head of broccoli, cut
into florets

2 tablespoons extra-virgin
olive oil

4 oz. Brussels sprouts, trimmed
and halved

½ teaspoon black pepper,
plus more to taste

1 large garlic clove, minced

1 teaspoon miso paste

⅔ cup mayonnaise

¼ cup buttermilk

¼ cup grated Parmesan cheese,
plus more for garnish

Zest of 1 lemon

1 teaspoon Worcestershire sauce

Red pepper flakes, for garnish

1   Bring a large pot of water to a boil. Add salt and the cauliflower, cook for 1 minute, remove with a slotted spoon, let the water drip off, and transfer to a paper towel–lined plate to drain. Wait for the water to return to a boil (if necessary), add the broccoli, and cook for 30 seconds. Use a slotted spoon to remove the broccoli and let the water drip off before transferring it to the paper towel–lined plate.

2   Place the oil and Brussels sprouts, cut side down, in a large cast-iron skillet. Add the broccoli and cauliflower, season with salt and pepper, and cook over high heat without moving the vegetables. Cook until charred, turn over, and cook until charred on that side. Remove and transfer to a salad bowl.

3   Place the garlic, miso, mayonnaise, buttermilk, Parmesan cheese, lemon zest, Worcestershire sauce, salt, and pepper in a food processor and puree until combined. Taste and adjust the seasoning as necessary.

4   Add the dressing to the salad bowl and toss to evenly coat. Garnish with additional Parmesan cheese and the red pepper flakes and serve.

GINGER & TAHINI SLAW

YIELD: **4 SERVINGS** / ACTIVE TIME: **15 MINUTES** / TOTAL TIME: **15 MINUTES**

INGREDIENTS

2 cups shredded green cabbage

2 cups shredded red cabbage

3 tablespoons chopped peanuts

3 scallions, trimmed and chopped

½ cup chopped fresh cilantro or parsley

1 cup tahini

1 teaspoon maple syrup

1 teaspoon grated fresh ginger

1 teaspoon rice vinegar

1 teaspoon toasted sesame oil

½ cup extra-virgin olive oil

1   Place the cabbages, peanuts, scallions, and cilantro or parsley in a salad bowl and toss to combine.

2   Place the remaining ingredients in a separate bowl and whisk vigorously until emulsified.

3   Add about ¼ cup of the dressing to the salad and toss. Taste and add more dressing if desired.

CORN FRITTERS

YIELD: **4 SERVINGS** / ACTIVE TIME: **20 MINUTES** / TOTAL TIME: **40 MINUTES**

INGREDIENTS

1 egg, beaten

1 teaspoon sugar

½ teaspoon kosher salt

1 tablespoon unsalted
butter, melted

2 teaspoons baking powder

1 cup all-purpose flour

⅔ cup milk

2 cups corn kernels, at room
temperature

¼ cup extra-virgin olive oil

1   Place the egg, sugar, salt, butter, baking powder, flour, and milk in a mixing bowl and stir until thoroughly combined. Add the corn and stir to incorporate.

2   Place the oil in a 12-inch cast-iron skillet and warm over medium-high heat. When the oil starts to shimmer, drop heaping spoonfuls of batter into the skillet. Make sure to not crowd the pan. Cook until the fritters are browned on both sides, about 3 minutes per side. Transfer to a paper towel–lined plate and tent with aluminum foil to keep warm while you cook the rest of the fritters. Serve once all of the fritters have been cooked.

NOTE: The best corn to use for this is leftover cooked corn on the cob that's been in the refrigerator over-night. Otherwise, you can take frozen corn and thaw the kernels, patting them dry before putting them in the batter. If you use canned corn, be sure all water is drained from it, and choose a high-quality brand so the kernels are firm and sweet, not mushy.

NEW POTATO CONFIT

YIELD: **6 SERVINGS** / ACTIVE TIME: **5 MINUTES** / TOTAL TIME: **1 HOUR**

INGREDIENTS

2 cups extra-virgin olive oil

5 lbs. new potatoes

Salt and pepper, to taste

1   Place the oil in a Dutch oven and bring it to 200°F over low heat.

2   While the oil is warming, wash the potatoes and pat them dry. Carefully place the potatoes in the oil and cook until fork-tender, about 1 hour.

3   Drain the potatoes, season generously with salt and pepper, and stir to ensure that the potatoes are evenly coated.

NOTE: These potatoes should have plenty of flavor, but if you're looking to take them to another level, replace the olive oil with chicken or duck fat.

BLISTERED SHISHITO PEPPERS

YIELD: **6 SERVINGS** / ACTIVE TIME: **5 MINUTES** / TOTAL TIME: **10 MINUTES**

INGREDIENTS

Extra-virgin olive oil, as needed

2 lbs. shishito peppers

Salt, to taste

1 lemon, cut into wedges,
for serving

1   Add olive oil to a large cast-iron skillet until it is ¼ inch deep and warm over medium heat.

2   When the oil is shimmering, add the peppers and cook, while turning once or twice, until they are blistered and golden brown, about 10 minutes. Take care not to crowd the pan with the peppers, and work in batches if necessary.

3   Transfer the blistered peppers to a paper towel–lined plate. Season with salt and serve with lemon wedges.

NOTE: Eating shishito peppers is a bit like putting your taste buds through a round of Russian roulette, since approximately one in every 10 is spicy, and there's no way to tell until you bite down. The rest are as mild as can be.

SAVORY HALWA

YIELD: **8 SERVINGS** / ACTIVE TIME: **15 MINUTES** / TOTAL TIME: **20 MINUTES**

INGREDIENTS

2 tablespoons unsalted butter

1 lb. carrots, peeled and grated

½ teaspoon cardamom

2 cups milk

Salt, to taste

1   Place the butter in a saucepan and melt over medium heat. Add the carrots and cardamom and cook until the carrots start to soften, about 5 minutes.

2   Add the milk, bring to a simmer, and cook until the milk has reduced by half and the carrots are very tender, about 10 minutes. Season with salt and serve.

POTATO & PARSNIP LATKES

YIELD: **4 SERVINGS** / ACTIVE TIME: **40 MINUTES** / TOTAL TIME: **1 HOUR**

INGREDIENTS

2 russet potatoes, peeled and grated

3 parsnips, peeled, trimmed, cored, and grated

1 tablespoon all-purpose flour

1 egg

Salt and pepper, to taste

3 tablespoons olive oil

Sour cream, for serving

Applesauce, for serving

1   Preheat the oven to 350°F. Place the grated potatoes in a colander and squeeze one handful at a time until no more liquid can be removed from them. Transfer to a bowl.

2   Add the parsnips, flour, and egg to the potatoes, stir to combine, and season with salt and pepper.

3   Place the oil in a large skillet and warm it over medium-high heat. When the oil starts to shimmer, add spoonfuls of the latke mixture to the pan and press down to flatten them into patties. Reduce the heat to medium-low and cook until brown on both sides, about 8 minutes per side.

4   When both sides are perfectly brown, test the latkes to see if the interiors are fully cooked. If not, place them on a baking sheet and bake in the oven for an additional 10 minutes. Let the cooked latkes cool briefly and then serve with sour cream and applesauce.

STUFFED MUSHROOMS

YIELD: **8 SERVINGS** / ACTIVE TIME: **30 MINUTES** / TOTAL TIME: **1 HOUR AND 30 MINUTES**

INGREDIENTS

10 oz. button mushrooms, stemmed

¼ cup extra-virgin olive oil, plus more as needed

3 tablespoons balsamic vinegar

Salt and pepper, to taste

4 hot Italian sausages, casings removed and crumbled

2 yellow onions, grated

5 garlic cloves, grated

½ lb. cream cheese, at room temperature

1 cup shredded Asiago cheese

1   Place the mushrooms, olive oil, and balsamic vinegar in a mixing bowl and toss to coat. Season the mixture with salt and pepper and then place it on a baking sheet. Place in the oven and bake until the mushrooms are just starting to turn brown, about 25 minutes. Remove from the oven and set them aside.

2   Coat the bottom of a large skillet with olive oil and warm it over medium heat. When the oil starts to shimmer, add the sausage and cook, breaking it up with a fork as it browns, until cooked through, about 6 minutes. Remove the sausage from the pan and place it in a mixing bowl.

3   Preheat the oven to 375°F. Place the onions in the skillet, reduce the heat to medium-low, and cook until dark brown, about 15 minutes. Stir in the garlic, sauté for 1 minute, and then add the mixture to the bowl containing the sausage. Add the cheeses to the bowl containing the sausage and stir to combine.

4   Arrange the mushrooms on the baking sheet so that their cavities are facing up. Fill the cavities with the sausage mixture, place the mushrooms in the oven, and bake until the cheese has melted and is golden brown, about 25 minutes. Remove from the oven and let cool slightly before serving.

CAPRESE SALAD

YIELD: **4 SERVINGS** / ACTIVE TIME: **15 MINUTES** / TOTAL TIME: **15 MINUTES**

INGREDIENTS

1 lb. heirloom tomatoes, sliced
(in season is a must)

Salt and pepper, to taste

1 lb. fresh mozzarella cheese,
sliced

¼ cup Basil Pesto (see page 11)

Highest quality extra-virgin
olive oil, to taste

1   Season the tomatoes with salt and pepper. While alternating, arrange them and the slices of mozzarella on a platter.

2   Drizzle the pesto and olive oil over the tomatoes and mozzarella and serve.

BEET RELISH

INGREDIENTS

4 red beets, trimmed and rinsed

1 large shallot, minced

2 teaspoons white wine vinegar

Salt and pepper, to taste

1 tablespoon red wine vinegar

2 tablespoons extra-virgin olive oil

1   Preheat the oven to 400°F. Place the beets in a baking dish, add a splash of water, cover the dish with aluminum foil, and place it in the oven. Roast the beets until they are so tender that a knife easily goes to the center when poked, about 45 minutes. Remove from the oven, remove the foil, and let the beets cool.

2   While the beets are in the oven, place the shallot and white wine vinegar in a mixing bowl, season the mixture with salt, and stir to combine. Let the mixture marinate.

3   Peel the beets, dice them, and place them in a mixing bowl. Add the remaining ingredients and the shallot mixture, season to taste, and serve.

ROASTED GARLIC

YIELD: **6 SERVINGS** / ACTIVE TIME: **15 MINUTES** / TOTAL TIME: **45 MINUTES**

INGREDIENTS

6 heads of garlic

Extra-virgin olive oil, as needed

Salt, to taste

1   Preheat the oven to 375°F. Cut the tops off each head of garlic and place them, cut side up, in a baking dish that is small enough for them to fit snugly. Add about ¼ inch of water to the dish, drizzle olive oil over the garlic, and sprinkle with salt.

2   Cover the dish with aluminum foil, place it in the oven, and roast for 20 minutes. Lift the foil and test to see if the cloves are soft. If not, re-cover the dish, add water if it has evaporated, and roast for another 10 minutes. Remove from the oven and, if desired, serve with Crostini (see page 82) and goat cheese.

FRIED SQUASH BLOSSOMS

YIELD: **6 SERVINGS** / ACTIVE TIME: **30 MINUTES** / TOTAL TIME: **45 MINUTES**

INGREDIENTS

Canola oil, as needed

1¼ cups all-purpose flour

1 teaspoon kosher salt, plus more to taste

12 oz. pilsner or club soda

24 zucchini blossoms, stamens removed

1   Add canola oil to a Dutch oven until it is approximately 2 inches deep and warm to 350°F over medium heat. Place the flour and salt in a bowl, add the beer or club soda, and stir until the batter is almost smooth.

2   Dredge the zucchini blossoms in the batter until coated. Working in batches so as not to crowd the pot, carefully lay the zucchini blossoms in the oil and fry until golden brown, 2 to 3 minutes, turning the blossoms over once as they fry. Remove from the oil with a slotted spoon, drain on a paper towel–lined plate, and season with salt. Serve warm.

ROASTED GRAPES

YIELD: **8 SERVINGS** / ACTIVE TIME: **10 MINUTES** / TOTAL TIME: **1 HOUR AND 30 MINUTES**

INGREDIENTS

2 lbs. red seedless grapes, rinsed and patted dry

Extra-virgin olive oil, as needed

Salt, to taste

1   Preheat the oven to 350°F. Place the grapes in a mixing bowl, drizzle olive oil generously over them, and toss to coat. Place the grapes on a baking sheet, season with salt, and place in the oven. Roast until most of the grapes have collapsed and are slightly charred, about 35 minutes.

2   Remove from the oven and let cool completely before serving—the longer you let the grapes sit, the more concentrated their flavor will become.

TIROPITAKIA

YIELD: **6 SERVINGS** / ACTIVE TIME: **45 MINUTES** / TOTAL TIME: **1 HOUR AND 15 MINUTES**

INGREDIENTS

½ lb. feta cheese

1 cup grated kefalotyri cheese

¼ cup finely chopped fresh parsley

2 eggs, beaten

Black pepper, to taste

1 (1 lb.) package of frozen phyllo dough, thawed

2 sticks of unsalted butter, melted

1   Place the feta in a mixing bowl and break it up with a fork. Add the kefalotyri, parsley, eggs, and pepper and stir to combine. Set the mixture aside.

2   Place 1 sheet of the phyllo dough on a large sheet of parchment paper. Gently brush the sheet with some of the melted butter, place another sheet on top, and brush this with more of the butter. Cut the phyllo dough into 2-inch-wide strips, place 1 teaspoon of the filling at the end of the strip closest to you, and fold one corner over to make a triangle. Fold the strip up until the filling is completely covered. Repeat with the remaining sheets of phyllo dough and filling.

3   Preheat the oven to 350°F and oil a baking sheet with some of the melted butter. Place the pastries on the baking sheet and bake in the oven until golden brown, about 15 minutes. Remove and let cool briefly before serving.

SCALLION PANCAKES

INGREDIENTS

1½ cups all-purpose flour, plus more as needed

¾ cup boiling water

7 tablespoons canola oil

1 tablespoon toasted sesame oil

1 teaspoon kosher salt

4 scallions, trimmed and sliced thin

1 Place the flour and the water in a mixing bowl and work the mixture until it holds together as a rough dough. Transfer the dough to a flour-dusted work surface and knead it until it is a tacky, nearly smooth ball. Cover the dough with plastic wrap and let it rest for 30 minutes.

2 Place 1 tablespoon of the canola oil, the sesame oil, and 1 tablespoon of flour in a small bowl and stir to combine. Set the mixture aside.

3 Divide the dough in half, cover one piece with plastic wrap, and set it aside. Place the other piece on a flour-dusted work surface and roll it into a 12-inch round. Drizzle approximately 1 tablespoon of the oil-and-flour mixture over the round and use a pastry brush to spread the mixture evenly. Sprinkle half of the salt and scallions over the round and roll it into a cylinder. Coil the cylinder into a spiral and flatten it with your palm. Cover with plastic wrap and repeat with the other piece of dough.

4 Warm a cast-iron skillet over low heat. Roll one piece of dough into a 9-inch round and make a slit, approximately ½ inch deep, in the center of the round. Cover with plastic wrap and repeat with the other piece of dough.

5   Coat the bottom of the skillet with some of the remaining oil and raise the heat to medium-low. When the oil is warm, place 1 pancake in the pan, cover it, and cook until the pancake is golden brown, about 1 minute. Drizzle oil over the pancake, use a pastry brush to spread it evenly, and carefully flip the pancake over. Cover the pan and cook until browned on that side, about 1 minute.

Remove the cover and cook the pancake until it is crisp and a deep golden brown, about 30 seconds. Flip it over and cook until crispy on that side, another 30 seconds. Remove from the pan, transfer to a wire rack to cool, and cook the other pancake. When both pancakes have been cooked, slice each one into wedges and serve.

MEXICAN STREET CORN

YIELD: **4 SERVINGS** / ACTIVE TIME: **25 MINUTES** / TOTAL TIME: **1 HOUR AND 15 MINUTES**

INGREDIENTS

6 ears of corn, in their husks

3 chipotles in adobo

½ cup mayonnaise

¼ cup sour cream

1½ tablespoons brown sugar

1 tablespoon fresh lime juice

2 tablespoons chopped fresh cilantro, plus more for garnish

1 teaspoon kosher salt, plus more to taste

½ teaspoon black pepper, plus more to taste

3 tablespoons extra-virgin olive oil

½ cup crumbled goat cheese

6 lime wedges, for serving

1   Preheat the oven to 400°F. Place the ears of corn on a baking sheet, place it in the oven, and roast the corn for about 25 minutes, until the kernels have a slight give to them. Remove from the oven and let the corn cool. When the ears of corn are cool enough to handle, husk them and set aside.

2   Preheat a gas or charcoal grill to medium heat (about 450°F). Place the chipotles, mayonnaise, sour cream, brown sugar, lime juice, cilantro, salt, and pepper in a food processor and puree until smooth. Set the mixture aside.

3   Drizzle the olive oil over the ears of corn, season them with salt and pepper, and place them on the grill. Cook, while turning, until they are charred all over, about 10 minutes.

4   Spread the chipotle mayonnaise over the ears of corn and sprinkle the goat cheese over them. Garnish with additional cilantro and serve with the wedges of lime.

FRIED BRUSSELS SPROUTS

YIELD: **4 SERVINGS** / ACTIVE TIME: **10 MINUTES** / TOTAL TIME: **15 MINUTES**

INGREDIENTS

¾ cup real maple syrup

½ cup apple cider vinegar

½ cup apple cider

Salt, to taste

Canola oil, as needed

1 lb. Brussels sprouts, trimmed and halved

1   Place the maple syrup, vinegar, apple cider, and a pinch of salt in a saucepan and cook, stirring constantly, over medium heat until the liquid has reduced by one-quarter. Remove the pan from heat and set it aside.

2   Add oil to a Dutch oven until it is about 3 inches deep. Warm it to 350°F, place the Brussels sprouts in the oil, and fry until they are crispy and browned, about 1 to 2 minutes. Transfer to a paper towel–lined plate to drain.

3   Place the Brussels sprouts in a bowl, season with salt, and add 1 tablespoon of the glaze for every cup of Brussels sprouts. Toss until evenly coated and serve.

NOTE: If you prefer not to deep-fry the Brussels sprouts, toss them with oil and salt and roast at 375°F for 20 minutes, until they are just tender.

CAULIFLOWER GRATIN

YIELD: **4 SERVINGS** / ACTIVE TIME: **20 MINUTES** / TOTAL TIME: **1 HOUR AND 15 MINUTES**

INGREDIENTS

2 cups white wine

2½ cups water

⅓ cup kosher salt

2 sticks of unsalted butter

6 garlic cloves, crushed

2 shallots, halved

1 cinnamon stick

3 whole cloves

1 teaspoon black peppercorns

1 sprig of fresh sage

2 sprigs of fresh thyme

1 head of cauliflower, trimmed

1 cup shredded Emmental cheese

¼ cup grated Parmesan cheese

1 Place all of the ingredients, except for the cauliflower and cheeses, in a large saucepan and bring to a boil. Reduce the heat so that the mixture gently simmers, add the head of cauliflower, and poach it until tender, about 30 minutes.

2 While the cauliflower is poaching, preheat the oven to 450°F. Transfer the cauliflower to a baking sheet, place it in the oven, and bake until the top is a deep golden brown, about 10 minutes.

3 Remove the cauliflower from the oven and spread the cheeses evenly over the top. Return to the oven and bake until the cheeses have browned. Remove from the oven and let cool slightly before slicing the cauliflower into quarters and serving.

STUFFED TOMATOES

YIELD: **6 SERVINGS** / ACTIVE TIME: **25 MINUTES** / TOTAL TIME: **1 HOUR**

INGREDIENTS

6 large tomatoes

Salt and pepper, to taste

1 tablespoon extra-virgin olive oil

1 red onion, chopped

4 garlic cloves, minced

½ green bell pepper, stemmed, seeded, and chopped

½ lb. ground turkey

1 teaspoon cumin

1 teaspoon chopped fresh marjoram

½ teaspoon allspice

½ teaspoon freshly grated nutmeg

2 teaspoons red pepper flakes

½ cup cooked long-grain rice

¼ cup chopped fresh parsley

¼ cup chopped fresh mint

1   Cut off the tops of the tomatoes and use a spoon to scoop out the insides. Sprinkle salt into the cavities and turn the tomatoes upside down on a paper towel–lined plate. Let them drain for 30 minutes.

2   Place the olive oil in a large cast-iron skillet and warm it over medium-high heat. When the oil starts to shimmer, add the onion, garlic, and bell pepper and cook, stirring frequently, until the onion is translucent, about 3 minutes. Add the turkey, cumin, marjoram, allspice, and nutmeg, season with salt and pepper, and cook, breaking the turkey up with a fork, until it is browned, about 8 minutes.

3   Set the oven's broiler to high. Transfer the mixture in the skillet to a mixing bowl, add the red pepper flakes, rice, parsley, and mint, and stir to combine. Fill the tomatoes' cavities with the mixture, wipe out the skillet, and arrange the tomatoes in the pan.

4   Place the stuffed tomatoes under the broiler and cook until the tops start to blister, about 5 minutes. Remove from the oven and serve immediately.

CELERIAC & TROUT REMOULADE

YIELD: **4 SERVINGS** / ACTIVE TIME: **10 MINUTES** / TOTAL TIME: **10 MINUTES**

INGREDIENTS

1 large celeriac, trimmed, peeled, and grated

Salt and white pepper, to taste

⅓ cup mayonnaise

Dash of Tabasco

1 teaspoon Dijon mustard

2 teaspoons fresh lemon juice

1 teaspoon capers

Bibb lettuce, as needed

4 oz. smoked trout, torn into large pieces

Fresh chives or parsley, chopped, for garnish

Lemon wedges, for serving

1   Bring a medium saucepan of water to a boil. Add salt and the celeriac and cook for 1 minute. Drain, rinse with cold water, and let it drain completely.

2   Place the mayonnaise, Tabasco, mustard, lemon juice, and capers in a bowl and stir to combine. Add the celeriac to the mayonnaise mixture, fold to incorporate, and season with salt and pepper.

3   Place a lettuce leaves on a serving plate, place the celeriac remoulade on top, and top with the smoked trout. Garnish with chives or parsley and serve with lemon wedges.

KALE CHIPS

YIELD: **4 SERVINGS** / ACTIVE TIME: **5 MINUTES** / TOTAL TIME: **15 MINUTES**

INGREDIENTS

1 bunch of kale, stemmed

1 teaspoon kosher salt

½ teaspoon black pepper

½ teaspoon paprika

½ teaspoon dried parsley

½ teaspoon dried basil

¼ teaspoon dried thyme

¼ teaspoon dried sage

2 tablespoons extra-virgin olive oil

1   Preheat the oven to 400°F. Tear the kale leaves into smaller pieces and place them in a mixing bowl. Add the remaining ingredients and work the mixture with your hands until the kale pieces are evenly coated.

2   Divide the seasoned kale between two parchment-lined baking sheets so that it sits on each in an even layer. Place in the oven and bake until crispy, 6 to 8 minutes. Remove and let cool before serving.

FRIED ARTICHOKE HEARTS

YIELD: **4 SERVINGS** / ACTIVE TIME: **20 MINUTES** / TOTAL TIME: **30 MINUTES**

INGREDIENTS

2 large artichokes

1 lemon, quartered

Extra-virgin olive oil, as needed

Salt, to taste

1   Prepare the artichokes by using a serrated knife to cut off the top half with the leaves and all but the last inch of the stem; continue whittling away the outer leaves until you see the hairy-looking choke within. Using a paring knife, peel the outer layer of the remaining part of the stem; cut the remaining artichoke into quarters and remove the hairy part in the middle. You should have the heart with a little bit of lower leaves left. Place in a bowl of water, add a squeeze of lemon juice, and set aside.

2   Bring water to a boil in a small saucepan. Add the artichokes and parboil until they begin to feel tender, about 3 to 5 minutes. Remove from the water, drain, and pat dry.

3   Place another small pot on the stove and fill with enough oil that the artichoke hearts will be submerged. Warm the oil over medium heat until it starts to sizzle.

4   Place the artichokes in the oil and fry until they are brown all over, turning occasionally, 8 to 10 minutes. Transfer to a paper towel–lined plate to drain. Season with salt and serve with the lemon wedges.

SPANISH POTATO TORTILLA

YIELD: **6 SERVINGS** / ACTIVE TIME: **30 MINUTES** / TOTAL TIME: **2 HOURS**

INGREDIENTS

5 large russet potatoes, peeled and sliced thin

1 Spanish onion, sliced

1 cup extra-virgin olive oil, plus more as needed

10 eggs, at room temperature

Large pinch of kosher salt

1   Preheat the oven to 350°F. Place the potatoes, onion, and olive oil in a large cast-iron skillet. The potatoes should be submerged. If not, add more oil as needed. Bring to a gentle simmer over low heat and cook until the potatoes are tender, about 30 minutes. Remove from heat and let cool slightly.

2   Use a slotted spoon to remove the potatoes and onion from the oil. Reserve the oil. Place the eggs and salt in a large bowl and whisk to combine. Add the potatoes and onion to the eggs.

3   Warm the skillet over high heat. Add ¼ cup of the reserved oil and swirl to coat the bottom and sides of the pan. Pour the egg-and-potato mixture into the pan and stir vigorously to ensure that the mixture does not stick to the sides. Cook for 1 minute and remove from heat. Place the pan over low heat, cover, and cook for 3 minutes.

4   Place the pan in the oven and cook until it is set. Remove from the oven and let it rest at room temperature for 1 hour.

5   To serve, turn the tortilla onto a plate and slice as desired.

Kefta, page 194

FROM LAND TO SEA

Most people are used to meat coming in portions that excite the eyes and palate and then sit like a rock in the stomach. Reducing the amount one consumes at a time removes this unpleasant aspect, allowing everyone to enjoy the rich flavors that chicken, beef, and pork make available.

The lightness and subtle flavors of seafood were made for a meal that utilizes the small-plate approach, and with preparations like an almost impossibly fresh-tasting Scallop Ceviche and the unpretentious fun of Takoyaki, you'll soon be nodding along in agreement.

CHICKEN SOUVLAKI

YIELD: **4 SERVINGS** / ACTIVE TIME: **20 MINUTES** / TOTAL TIME: **2 HOURS AND 30 MINUTES**

INGREDIENTS

10 garlic cloves, crushed

4 sprigs of fresh oregano

1 sprig of fresh rosemary

1 teaspoon paprika

1 teaspoon kosher salt

1 teaspoon black pepper

¼ cup extra-virgin olive oil, plus
more as needed

¼ cup dry white wine

2 tablespoons fresh lemon juice

2½ lbs. boneless, skinless
chicken breasts, chopped

2 bay leaves

1   Place the garlic, oregano, rosemary, paprika, salt, pepper, olive oil, wine, and lemon juice in a food processor and blitz to combine. Place the chicken and bay leaves in a bowl or a large resealable bag, pour the marinade over the chicken, and stir so that it gets evenly coated. Refrigerate for 2 hours, stirring or shaking occasionally.

2   Remove the chicken from the refrigerator, thread the pieces onto skewers, and allow them to come to room temperature. Prepare a gas or charcoal grill for medium heat (about 450°F).

3   Place the skewers on the grill and cook, turning frequently, until the chicken is cooked through, 6 to 8 minutes. Remove the skewers from the grill and let them rest for 10 minutes before serving.

CHICKEN 65

YIELD: **6 SERVINGS** / ACTIVE TIME: **1 HOUR** / TOTAL TIME: **2 HOURS**

INGREDIENTS

1 lb. boneless, skinless chicken thighs, chopped

1 teaspoon mashed fresh ginger

2 garlic cloves, minced

½ teaspoon chili powder, plus more to taste

1 teaspoon fresh lemon juice

½ teaspoon black pepper, plus more to taste

⅛ teaspoon turmeric

Salt, to taste

2 tablespoons cornstarch

1 tablespoon rice flour

Canola oil, as needed

½ teaspoon sugar

2 tablespoons plain yogurt

1 tablespoon butter

3 to 5 curry leaves

2 green chili peppers, stemmed, seeded, and chopped

½ teaspoon cumin

1 Rinse the chicken and pat it dry. Place the ginger, 1 teaspoon of the garlic, the chili powder, lemon juice, black pepper, turmeric, and salt in a mixing bowl and stir to combine. Add the chicken and stir to coat. Place in the refrigerator and marinate for at least 1 hour.

2 When ready to cook the chicken, place the cornstarch and flour in a mixing bowl, stir to combine, and dredge the marinated chicken in the mixture.

3 Add canola oil to a Dutch oven until it is 2 inches deep and warm it to 350°F over medium heat. Place the sugar, remaining garlic, and yogurt in a mixing bowl, season with chili powder and salt, and stir to combine. Set the mixture aside.

4 Working in batches if necessary to avoid crowding the pot, place the chicken in the oil and fry until golden brown and cooked through, about 8 minutes. Remove the cooked chicken from the pot and let it drain on a paper towel–lined plate.

5 Place the butter, curry leaves, chilies, and cumin in a small pan and cook, stirring frequently, over medium heat until fragrant. Stir in the yogurt mixture and bring the sauce to a simmer. Add the fried chicken to the sauce and cook until the chicken has absorbed most of the liquid. Let cool briefly before serving.

POPCORN CHICKEN

YIELD: **4 SERVINGS** / ACTIVE TIME: **25 MINUTES** / TOTAL TIME: **1 HOUR AND 30 MINUTES**

INGREDIENTS

3 garlic cloves, smashed

1 egg white

1 tablespoon soy sauce

1½ tablespoons sesame oil

½ teaspoon white pepper

1 tablespoon cornstarch

Salt, to taste

1 lb. boneless, skin-on chicken breast, cut into bite-sized pieces

7 tablespoons tapioca starch, plus more as needed

2 cups canola oil

1 Place the garlic, egg white, soy sauce, sesame oil, white pepper, cornstarch, and salt in a mixing bowl and stir to combine. Add the chicken, toss to coat, and cover the bowl. Chill in the refrigerator for 1 hour.

2 Dust a baking sheet with tapioca starch, add the chicken, and turn it in the starch until it is coated, adding more tapioca starch as necessary.

3 Place the canola oil in a Dutch oven and warm it to 350°F over medium heat. Shake the chicken to remove any excess starch, add it to the pot in batches, and fry until golden brown. Make sure you do not overcrowd the pot. Place the cooked chicken on a paper towel–lined plate to drain and briefly let it cool before serving.

CONFIT DUCK LEGS

YIELD: **6 SERVINGS** / ACTIVE TIME: **30 MINUTES** / TOTAL TIME: **2 HOURS AND 30 MINUTES**

INGREDIENTS

6 duck legs

Salt, to taste

1 tablespoon extra-virgin olive oil

1. Pat the duck legs dry with paper towels and season them generously with salt. With the tip of a knife, gently poke the skin all around each leg. This will help release the fat as it renders. Let the legs rest at room temperature for at least 25 minutes.

2. Coat the bottom of a Dutch oven with the olive oil, add the duck legs, and set the oven to 285°F. Place the Dutch oven, uncovered, in the oven. You do not want to preheat the oven, as starting the duck at a low temperature allows its fat to render.

3. After 1½ hours, check the duck. It should be under a layer of duck fat and the skin should be getting crisp. If the legs aren't browned and crispy, let the duck cook longer. When the skin is starting to crisp, raise the oven's temperature to 375°F and cook the duck for another 15 minutes.

4. Remove the pot from the oven, remove the duck legs from the fat, and let them rest for 10 minutes before serving.

SOUTHWESTERN SLIDERS

YIELD: **6 SERVINGS** / ACTIVE TIME: **20 MINUTES** / TOTAL TIME: **35 MINUTES**

INGREDIENTS

1 large egg

2 chipotles in adobo

2 tablespoons whole milk

½ cup bread crumbs

½ cup grated jalapeño jack cheese

3 tablespoons finely chopped fresh cilantro

3 tablespoons canned diced green chilies, drained

4 garlic cloves, minced

1 tablespoon dried oregano

1 tablespoon smoked paprika

2 teaspoons cumin

1¼ lbs. ground beef

Salt and pepper, to taste

Slider rolls, for serving

1 Preheat a gas or charcoal grill to medium heat (450°F). Place the egg, chipotles, milk, and bread crumbs in a food processor and puree until smooth. Place the mixture in a mixing bowl, add the cheese, cilantro, green chilies, garlic, oregano, paprika, and cumin and stir until thoroughly combined.

2 Stir in the beef and season the mixture with salt and pepper. Working with wet hands, form the mixture into 3-inch patties. Place the sliders on the grill and cook until cooked through, about 10 minutes. Remove from the grill, transfer to a platter, and tent loosely with aluminum foil.

3 Let the sliders rest for 10 minutes before serving with the slider rolls and your favorite burger fixings.

KEFTA

YIELD: **4 SERVINGS** / ACTIVE TIME: **35 MINUTES** / TOTAL TIME: **1 HOUR**

INGREDIENTS

1½ lbs. ground lamb

½ lb. ground beef

½ white onion, minced

2 garlic cloves, roasted and mashed

Zest of 1 lemon

1 cup fresh parsley, chopped

2 tablespoons chopped fresh mint

1 teaspoon cinnamon

2 tablespoons cumin

1 tablespoon paprika

1 teaspoon coriander

Salt and pepper, to taste

¼ cup extra-virgin olive oil

1   Place all of the ingredients, except for the olive oil, in a mixing bowl and stir until well combined. Place a small bit of the mixture in a skillet and cook over medium heat until cooked through. Taste and adjust the seasoning in the remaining mixture as necessary. Working with wet hands, form the mixture into 18 ovals and place three meatballs on a skewer.

2   Place the olive oil in a Dutch oven and warm it over medium-high heat. Working in batches, add three skewers to the pot and sear the kefta until browned all over and nearly cooked through. Transfer the browned kefta to a paper towel–lined plate to drain.

3   When all of the kefta has been browned, return all of the skewers to the pot, cover it, and remove from heat. Let stand for 10 minutes so the kefta get cooked through.

4   When the kefta are cooked through, remove them from the skewers and serve.

CARNE ASADA

YIELD: **4 SERVINGS** / ACTIVE TIME: **20 MINUTES** / TOTAL TIME: **7 HOURS**

INGREDIENTS

1 lb. skirt steak

2 tablespoons extra-virgin
olive oil

Juice of 1 lime

Salt, to taste

1 teaspoon cumin

1 teaspoon smoked paprika

2 teaspoons ancho chile powder

1½ oz. mezcal

1   Using a sharp knife, slice the steak across the grain into very thin strips. Place the strips in a large bowl.

2   In a separate bowl, combine the remaining ingredients, except for the mezcal. Pour the marinade over the sliced steak and rub it into the meat with your hands. Cover the bowl and let the steak marinate in the refrigerator for 6 hours.

3   Remove the steak from the refrigerator and let it come to room temperature.

4   Stir the mezcal into the marinade. Place a large cast-iron skillet over high heat. When the pan is ripping hot, let the excess marinade drip off the steak and spread it in an even layer in the skillet. Cook until the steak is well charred, about 5 minutes per side. Remove from the pan and let the steak rest for 10 minutes before serving with tortillas.

NOTE: Placing the meat in the freezer for 20 minutes before slicing will make it easier to cut it thin.

MASALA SHORT RIB SANDWICHES

YIELD: **6 SERVINGS** / ACTIVE TIME: **45 MINUTES** / TOTAL TIME: **3 HOURS**

INGREDIENTS

3 lbs. bone-in short ribs

Salt and pepper, to taste

1 tablespoon extra-virgin olive oil

1 onion, sliced

5 garlic cloves, minced

1 teaspoon grated fresh ginger

1 lb. tomatoes, chopped

1 teaspoon cumin

1 teaspoon curry powder

1 teaspoon garam masala

½ teaspoon cayenne pepper

1 teaspoon coriander

4 cups Beef Stock (see sidebar)

Rolls, for serving

1. Season the short ribs generously with salt. Place the olive oil in a Dutch oven and warm it over medium-high heat. When the oil begins to shimmer, add the short ribs and cook until browned all over, 2 to 3 minutes per side. Work in batches if necessary to avoid crowding the pot. Remove the browned short ribs and set them aside.

2. Add the onion to the pot and cook, stirring frequently, until it begins to brown, about 4 minutes. Stir in the garlic, ginger, and tomatoes, cook for 1 minute, and then add the cumin, curry, garam masala, cayenne, and coriander.

3. Deglaze the pot with the stock, using a wooden spoon to scrape up the browned bits from the bottom. Cook until the stock has reduced by half.

4. Return the short ribs to the pot, cover it, and reduce the heat until the mixture simmers. Cook for about 2 hours, until the meat is extremely tender.

5. Remove the short ribs from the pot and let them rest for 20 minutes. Remove the bone and assemble the sandwiches using the rolls.

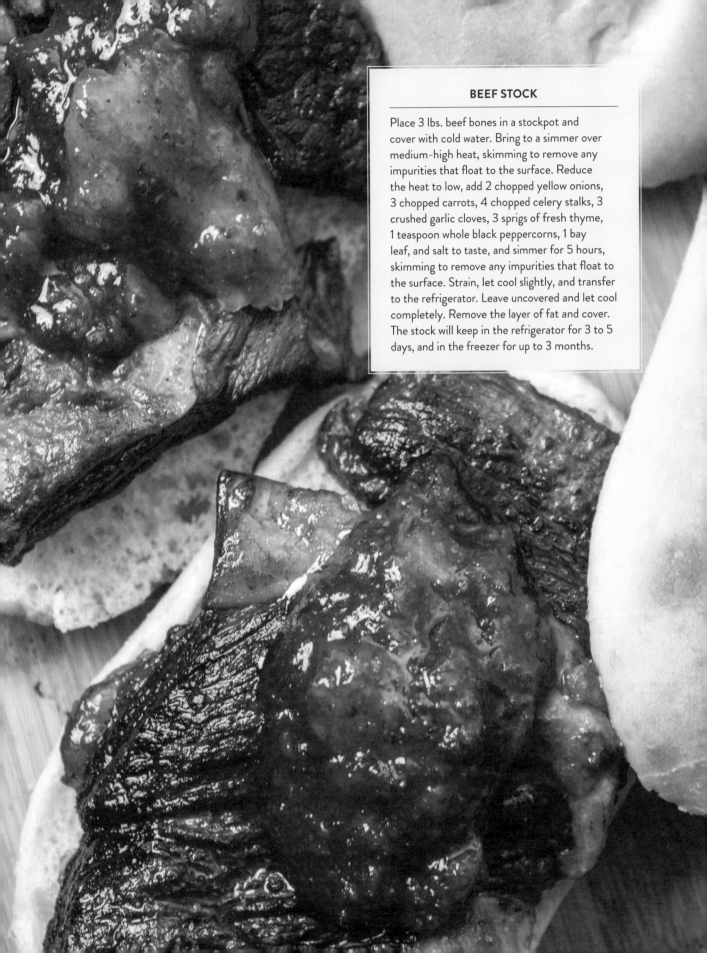

BEEF STOCK

Place 3 lbs. beef bones in a stockpot and cover with cold water. Bring to a simmer over medium-high heat, skimming to remove any impurities that float to the surface. Reduce the heat to low, add 2 chopped yellow onions, 3 chopped carrots, 4 chopped celery stalks, 3 crushed garlic cloves, 3 sprigs of fresh thyme, 1 teaspoon whole black peppercorns, 1 bay leaf, and salt to taste, and simmer for 5 hours, skimming to remove any impurities that float to the surface. Strain, let cool slightly, and transfer to the refrigerator. Leave uncovered and let cool completely. Remove the layer of fat and cover. The stock will keep in the refrigerator for 3 to 5 days, and in the freezer for up to 3 months.

SWEDISH MEATBALLS

YIELD: **6 SERVINGS** / ACTIVE TIME: **20 MINUTES** / TOTAL TIME: **45 MINUTES**

INGREDIENTS

4 tablespoons unsalted butter

1 small onion, chopped

¼ cup milk

1 large egg

1 large egg yolk

3 slices of white bread

¼ teaspoon allspice

¼ teaspoon freshly grated nutmeg

Pinch of ground ginger

¾ lb. ground pork

½ lb. ground beef

Salt and pepper, to taste

¼ cup all-purpose flour

2½ cups Chicken Stock (see page 123)

½ cup heavy cream

1   Preheat the broiler to high, position a rack so that the tops of the meatballs will be approximately 6 inches below the broiler, and line a rimmed baking sheet with aluminum foil.

2   Place 2 tablespoons of the butter in a large skillet and melt it over medium-high heat. Add the onion and cook, stirring frequently, until it is translucent, about 3 minutes. Remove the pan from heat and set it aside.

3   Place the milk, egg, and egg yolk in a mixing bowl and stir to combine. Tear the bread into small pieces and add them to mixing bowl along with the allspice, nutmeg, and ginger. Stir in the pork, beef, and the onion, season the mixture with salt and pepper, and stir until thoroughly combined. Working with wet hands, form the mixture into 1½-inch meatballs, arrange them on the baking sheet, and spray the tops with nonstick cooking spray.

4   Place the meatballs in the oven and broil until browned all over, turning them as they cook. Remove the meatballs from the oven and set them aside.

5   Place the remaining butter in the skillet and melt it over low heat. Add the flour, cook for 2 minutes while stirring constantly, and then raise the heat to medium-high. Stir in the stock and cream and bring to a boil.

6   Add the meatballs to the sauce, reduce the heat to low, cover the pan, and simmer, turning the meatballs occasionally, until they are cooked through, about 15 minutes. Season with salt and pepper and serve.

CORN DOGS

YIELD: **4 SERVINGS** / ACTIVE TIME: **20 MINUTES** / TOTAL TIME: **1 HOUR**

INGREDIENTS

1 cup cornmeal

1 cup all-purpose flour

2 teaspoons kosher salt

¼ cup sugar

4 teaspoons baking powder

1 egg white

1 cup milk

Canola oil, as needed

4 hot dogs

1   Soak four bamboo skewers in water for 30 minutes. Place the cornmeal, flour, salt, sugar, and baking powder in a mixing bowl and stir to combine. Place the egg white and milk in a separate bowl and whisk to combine. Add the wet mixture to the dry mixture and stir until thoroughly combined.

2   Add oil to a Dutch oven until it is approximately 2 inches deep and warm it to 350°F over medium heat. Skewer the hot dogs and roll them in the batter until well coated. When the oil is at the correct temperature, add the corn dogs and fry until golden brown, about 3 minutes.

CHAR SIU

YIELD: **6 SERVINGS** / ACTIVE TIME: **40 MINUTES** / TOTAL TIME: **24 HOURS**

INGREDIENTS

2 pieces of fermented
red bean curd

1 tablespoon honey

1 tablespoon Shaoxing wine

1 tablespoon soy sauce

1 tablespoon oyster sauce

1 teaspoon dark soy sauce

1 teaspoon five-spice powder

¼ teaspoon white pepper

½ cup sugar

2 garlic cloves, minced

1 lb. skinless pork belly, cut into
2 long strips

1   Place all of the ingredients, except for the garlic and pork belly, in a mixing bowl and stir until combined. Place the garlic and pork belly in a mixing bowl, add half of the sauce, and stir until the pork belly is coated. Refrigerate the pork belly, uncovered, and the remaining sauce overnight.

2   Preheat the oven to 400°F. Remove the pork belly and reserved sauce from the refrigerator and let them come to room temperature. Place the pork belly on a wire rack in a rimmed baking sheet lined with aluminum foil, place it in the oven, and roast it for 15 minutes.

3   Remove the pork belly from the oven, turn it over, and brush some of the reserved sauce over it. Return the pork belly to the oven and roast for another 15 minutes.

4   Set the oven's broiler to high and broil the pork belly on each side until they are charred, about 1 minute per side. Remove the pork belly from the oven and let it rest.

5   Place the remaining sauce over medium heat and bring to a simmer over medium-low heat. When the pork belly has rested for 15 minutes, slice it into bite-sized pieces and serve it alongside the warmed sauce.

CRAB RANGOONS

YIELD: **6 SERVINGS** / ACTIVE TIME: **25 MINUTES** / TOTAL TIME: **45 MINUTES**

INGREDIENTS

1 lb. cream cheese, at room temperature

6 oz. fresh crabmeat

2 tablespoons confectioners' sugar

¼ teaspoon kosher salt

40 wonton wrappers (see page 218)

Canola oil, as needed

1   Place the cream cheese, crabmeat, sugar, and salt in a medium bowl and fold to combine. Place about 1 tablespoon of the filling in the middle of a wrapper. Rub the wrapper's edge with a wet finger, bring the corners together, pinch to seal tightly, and transfer to a parchment-lined baking sheet. Repeat with the remaining wrappers and filling.

2   Add oil to a Dutch oven until it is 2 inches deep and warm it to 325°F over medium heat. Working in batches of six to eight, gently slip the wontons into the hot oil and fry, while turning, until golden brown all over, about 3 minutes. Transfer the cooked rangoons to a paper towel–lined wire rack and repeat with the remaining dumplings. Let cool briefly before serving.

SCALLOP CEVICHE

YIELD: **4 SERVINGS** / ACTIVE TIME: **10 MINUTES** / TOTAL TIME: **20 MINUTES**

INGREDIENTS

Pinch of kosher salt

Juice of 1 lime

½ shallot, diced

1 tablespoon sliced scallions

1 teaspoon honey

2 fresh mint leaves, chopped

1 teaspoon chopped
jalapeño pepper

½ teaspoon pomegranate
molasses

Dash of white vinegar

6 large scallops

1   Place all of the ingredients, except for the scallops, in a mixing bowl and stir to combine. Let the marinade sit for 15 minutes.

2   Using a very sharp knife, cut the scallops into round, ⅛-inch-thick slices. Add the scallops to the marinade and gently stir. In a minute or two, your scallops should cure and turn completely white. Serve immediately.

TURMERIC & GINGER SHRIMP

YIELD: **8 SERVINGS** / ACTIVE TIME: **30 MINUTES** / TOTAL TIME: **2 HOURS AND 30 MINUTES**

INGREDIENTS

1-inch piece of fresh ginger,
peeled and grated

2 garlic cloves, minced

1-inch piece of fresh turmeric,
peeled and grated

2 tablespoons chopped scallions

1 shallot, minced

Juice of 1 lime

Juice of 1 scallion

1 tablespoon kosher salt

1 teaspoon honey

1 tablespoon extra-virgin olive oil

1 lb. large shrimp, peeled and
deveined

1 Place all of the ingredients, except for the shrimp, in a mixing bowl and stir to combine. Add the shrimp, stir until coated, and cover the bowl. Place the bowl in the refrigerator and let the shrimp marinate for at least 2, and up to 6, hours.

2 Warm a large skillet over medium-high heat. When the skillet is warm, add the shrimp and marinade and cook until the shrimp are pink, about 2 minutes. Take care not to crowd the pan, and work in batches if necessary. Serve warm or at room temperature.

NOTE: If fresh turmeric is not available, substitute 1 teaspoon of turmeric powder.

LOBSTER TOSTADAS

YIELD: **4 SERVINGS** / ACTIVE TIME: **20 MINUTES** / TOTAL TIME: **1 HOUR AND 30 MINUTES**

INGREDIENTS

1 (14 oz.) can of corn, drained

1 small jalapeño pepper, stemmed, seeded, and diced, plus more for garnish

¼ cup diced red onion

1 garlic clove, minced

1½ tablespoons fresh lime juice

¼ cup chopped fresh cilantro, plus more for garnish

½ cup diced tomato

Salt and pepper, to taste

2 cups canola oil

8 corn tortillas

Paprika, to taste

Sour cream, to taste

Meat from 4 cooked chicken lobsters

Red cabbage, sliced thin, for garnish

Lime wedges, for serving

1   Place the corn, jalapeño, onion, garlic, lime juice, cilantro, and tomato in a mixing bowl and stir to combine. Season with salt and pepper and set the mixture aside.

2   Place the canola oil in a Dutch oven and warm to 350°F over medium heat. Working with one tortilla at a time, place them into the oil and fry until golden brown. Remove from the oil, transfer to a paper towel–lined plate, and season with salt and paprika.

3   Spread some sour cream on each tortilla and top it with the corn mixture and lobster meat. Garnish the tostadas with red cabbage, jalapeño, and cilantro and serve with lime wedges.

CRAB CAKES

YIELD: **6 SERVINGS** / ACTIVE TIME: **35 MINUTES** / TOTAL TIME: **1 HOUR AND 45 MINUTES**

INGREDIENTS

1 lb. jumbo lump crabmeat, picked over

4 scallion greens, minced

1 tablespoon chopped fresh parsley

1½ teaspoons Old Bay seasoning

2 tablespoons bread crumbs, plus more as needed

¼ cup mayonnaise

1 large egg

½ cup all-purpose flour

6 tablespoons extra-virgin olive oil

1   Place the crabmeat, scallions, parsley, Old Bay, bread crumbs, and mayonnaise in a mixing bowl and fold to combine. Season with salt and pepper, add the egg, and fold until the mixture starts holding together. If the mixture is struggling to hold together, incorporate more bread crumbs, a pinch at a time.

2   Form heaping tablespoons of the mixture into cakes and place them on a parchment-lined baking sheet. Refrigerate for 1 hour.

3   Preheat the oven to 200°F and place a parchment-lined baking sheet in it. Place the flour in a shallow bowl, dredge the crab cakes in the flour, and gently shake them to remove any excess. Coat the bottom of a large skillet with some of the olive oil and warm it over medium-high heat. When the oil starts to shimmer, add the crab cakes and cook until brown and crisp on both sides, 1 to 2 minutes per side. Cook the crab cakes in batches and add oil to the pan if it starts to look dry. Transfer the cooked crab cakes to the baking sheet in the oven to keep them warm. Serve once all of the crab cakes have been cooked.

TAKOYAKI SAUCE

Place ½ cup Worcestershire sauce, 1 tablespoon mentsuyu or chicken stock, 2¼ teaspoons sugar, and 1½ teaspoons ketchup in a small bowl and stir to combine. Taste, adjust the seasoning as necessary, and use as desired.

TAKOYAKI

YIELD: **4 SERVINGS** / ACTIVE TIME: **20 MINUTES** / TOTAL TIME: **20 MINUTES**

INGREDIENTS

2 teaspoons sake

2 teaspoons mirin

2 teaspoons soy sauce

2 teaspoons oyster sauce

2 teaspoons Worcestershire sauce

1 tablespoon sugar

1 tablespoon ketchup

Salt and white pepper, to taste

2 tablespoons water, plus more as needed

1 large egg

1½ cups Chicken Stock (see page 123)

¾ cup all-purpose flour

1 cup minced cooked octopus

2 scallion greens, sliced thin

¼ cup minced pickled ginger

Takoyaki Sauce (see sidebar), for serving

1 Place the sake, mirin, soy sauce, oyster sauce, Worcestershire sauce, sugar, ketchup, salt, and white pepper in a mixing bowl and stir to combine. Set the mixture aside.

2 Place the water, the egg, and stock in a bowl and stir until combined. Sprinkle the flour over the mixture and stir until all of the flour has been incorporated and the mixture is a thick batter. Add the sake-and-mirin mixture and stir to incorporate. Pour the batter into a measuring cup with a spout.

3 Coat the wells of an aebleskiver pan or a muffin pan with nonstick cooking spray and place it over medium heat. When the pan is hot, fill the wells of the pan halfway and add a pinch of octopus, scallion, and pickled ginger to each. Fill the wells the rest of the way with the batter, until they are almost overflowing. Cook the dumplings for approximately 2 minutes and use a chopstick to flip each one over. Turn the fritters as needed until they are golden brown on both sides and piping hot. Serve immediately alongside the Takoyaki Sauce.

MAINE LOBSTER WONTONS

YIELD: **4 TO 6 SERVINGS** / ACTIVE TIME: **45 MINUTES** / TOTAL TIME: **3 HOURS MINUTES**

1   To begin preparations for the wrappers, place the water, egg, and salt in a measuring cup and whisk to combine. Place the flour in the bowl of a stand mixer fitted with the paddle attachment. With the mixer running on low speed, add the egg mixture in a steady stream and beat until the dough holds together. Add water or flour in ½-teaspoon increments if the dough is too dry or too wet, respectively. Fit the mixer with the dough hook and knead at medium speed until the dough is soft, smooth, and springs back quickly when pressed with a finger, about 10 minutes. Cover the dough tightly with plastic wrap and let it rest for 2 hours.

2   Cut the dough into three even pieces. Working with one piece at a time (cover the others tightly in plastic wrap), shape the dough into a ball. Place the dough on a flour-dusted work surface and roll it out to ½ inch thick. Feed the dough through a pasta maker, adjusting the setting to reduce the thickness with each pass, until the dough

is about ¹⁄₁₆ inch thick, thin enough that you can see your hand through it. Place the sheets on the work surface, roll out to 6 inches long, and place the sheets on a parchment-lined baking sheet.

3   Dust a work surface with cornstarch and cut the sheets into as many 4-inch squares as possible.

4   To prepare the filling, place all of the ingredients, except for the egg, in a mixing bowl and fold to combine. Place 1 tablespoon of the mixture in the center of a wrapper. Dip a finger into the beaten egg and rub it around the edge of the wrapper. Bring the corners together to make a purse and seal closed. Repeat with the remaining wrappers and filling.

5   Bring water to boil in a large pot. Working in batches, place the wontons in the boiling water and cook for 3 minutes. Remove and serve immediately.

INGREDIENTS

FOR THE WRAPPERS

¼ cup water, plus more
as needed

1 large egg

¾ teaspoon fine sea salt

1½ cups all-purpose flour, plus
more as needed

Cornstarch, as needed

FOR THE FILLING

1½ cups minced
Maine lobster meat

½ shallot, minced

¼ teaspoon minced fresh ginger

¼ teaspoon minced garlic

1 teaspoon fish sauce

2 tablespoons heavy cream

2 tablespoons chopped
fresh chives

Salt and pepper, to taste

1 egg, beaten

PUB SARDINES

YIELD: **4 SERVINGS** / ACTIVE TIME: **5 MINUTES** / TOTAL TIME: **10 MINUTES**

INGREDIENTS

1 tablespoon sake

1 tablespoon soy sauce

1 can of sardines in olive oil, drained

Pinch of black pepper

2 teaspoons sansho peppercorns

1   Add the sake and soy sauce to the can of sardines.

2   Top with the black pepper and sansho peppercorns.

3   Place the can directly on a burner, cook over the lowest heat for 4 to 5 minutes, and serve.

DESSERTS

One benefit of keeping things small when it comes time to make a meal is that you have enough room to conclude with something sweet. These confections are made for such endings, remaining in line with the emphasis on ease, simplicity, and deliciousness that has been established in the preceding chapters.

SWEET TART SHELL

YIELD: **1 TART SHELL** / ACTIVE TIME: **30 MINUTES** / TOTAL TIME: **3 HOURS AND 15 MINUTES**

INGREDIENTS

1 large egg yolk

1 tablespoon heavy cream

½ teaspoon pure vanilla extract

1¼ cups all-purpose flour, plus
more as needed

⅔ cup confectioners' sugar

¼ teaspoon kosher salt

1 stick of unsalted butter, cut
into 4 pieces

1   Place the egg yolk, cream, and vanilla in a small bowl, whisk to combine, and set aside. Place the flour, sugar, and salt in a food processor and pulse to combine. Add the pieces of butter and pulse until the mixture resembles a coarse meal. Set the food processor to puree and add the egg mixture as it is running. Puree until the dough just comes together, about 20 seconds. Place the dough on a sheet of plastic wrap, press down to flatten it into 6-inch disk, wrap, and refrigerate for 2 hours.

2   Approximately 1 hour before you are planning to start constructing your tart, remove the dough from the refrigerator. Lightly dust a large sheet of parchment paper with flour and place the dough in the center. Roll out to 9 inches and line the tart pan with it. Place the pan containing the rolled-out dough in the freezer.

3   Preheat the oven to 375°F. Place the chilled tart shell on cookie sheet, line the inside of the tart shell with aluminum foil, and fill with uncooked rice, dried beans, or pie weights. Bake for 30 minutes, rotating the shell halfway through.

4   After 30 minutes, remove the shell from the oven and discard the foil and weight. Leave the tart shell on the cookie sheet and place it on the upper rack of the oven. Bake until the shell is golden brown, about 5 minutes. Remove and fill as desired.

CARAMELIZED PEACH CUSTARD TART

YIELD: **8 SERVINGS** / ACTIVE TIME: **25 MINUTES** / TOTAL TIME: **1 HOUR**

INGREDIENTS

2 tablespoons unsalted butter

2 large peaches, pitted and sliced

7 tablespoons sugar

¼ teaspoon cinnamon

2 tablespoons brandy

½ cup milk

½ cup heavy cream

2 eggs

1 egg yolk

½ teaspoon pure vanilla extract

¼ teaspoon fine sea salt

1 Sweet Tart Shell (see page 225)

1   Place the butter in a skillet and melt over medium-high heat. Add the peaches to the melted butter and cook, turning the slices as needed, until they are brown all over, about 8 minutes.

2   Sprinkle 3 tablespoons of the sugar over the peaches and shake the pan until they are evenly coated. Cook until the peaches start to caramelize, about 10 minutes.

3   Remove the pan from heat and tilt it away from you. Add the brandy and use a long match or a long-handled lighter to ignite the brandy. Place the pan back on the stove and cook, while shaking the pan, until the alcohol cooks off. Pour the mixture into a heatproof mixing bowl and let it cool.

4   Preheat the oven to 300°F. When the flambéed peaches are close to cool, place the milk, heavy cream, eggs, egg yolk, remaining sugar, vanilla, and salt in a mixing bowl and whisk to combine.

5   Distribute the flambéed peaches in the tart shell and then strain the custard over the top. Place the tart in the oven and bake until the custard is just set, 20 to 25 minutes. Remove from the oven and let cool before serving.

ROSÉ SORBET

YIELD: **6 SERVINGS** / ACTIVE TIME: **10 MINUTES** / TOTAL TIME: **24 HOURS**

INGREDIENTS

1⅓ cups sugar

1 (750 ml) bottle of Rosé

1 cup water

1　Place all of the ingredients in a saucepan and cook, while stirring, over medium-low heat until the sugar is completely dissolved. Raise the heat and bring to a boil.

2　Remove from heat and let cool completely. Cover and place the mixture in the refrigerator overnight.

3　Pour the mixture into an ice cream maker and churn until the desired texture has been achieved.

4　Transfer the sorbet to the freezer and freeze for at least 4 hours before serving.

NOTE: An ice cream maker is a must for this preparation. While not an essential kitchen appliance, a more-than-serviceable one from Cuisinart is available for around $40.

DATE & TOFFEE PUDDING CAKES

YIELD: **8 SERVINGS** / ACTIVE TIME: **45 MINUTES** / TOTAL TIME: **1 HOUR AND 30 MINUTES**

INGREDIENTS

¾ cup warm water (110°F)

½ teaspoon baking soda

½ lb. pitted dates, chopped

1¼ cups all-purpose flour

½ teaspoon baking powder

¾ teaspoon fine sea salt

1¾ cups firmly packed dark brown sugar

2 large eggs

1 stick of unsalted butter, half melted, half at room temperature

1½ tablespoons pure vanilla extract

1 cup heavy cream

Dash of fresh lemon juice

1   Place the water, baking soda, and half of the dates in a large mason jar and soak for 5 minutes. Make sure the liquid is covering the dates.

2   Preheat the oven to 350°F and coat eight 4 oz. ramekins with nonstick cooking spray. Bring water to a boil in a small saucepan.

3   Place the flour, baking powder, and ½ teaspoon of the salt in a mixing bowl and whisk to combine.

4   Place ¾ cup of the brown sugar and the remaining dates in a blender or food processor and blitz until the mixture is fine. Drain the soaked dates, reserve the liquid, and set the dates aside. Add the reserved liquid to the blender along with the eggs, melted butter, and vanilla and puree until smooth. Add the puree and soaked dates to the flour mixture and fold to combine.

5   Fill each ramekin two-thirds of the way with the batter, place the filled ramekins in a large roasting pan, and pour the boiling water in the roasting pan so that it goes halfway up the side of each ramekin.

6   Cover tightly with aluminum foil and place the pan in the oven. Bake until each cake is puffy and the surfaces are spongy but firm, about 40 minutes. Remove the ramekins from the roasting pan and let cool on a wire rack for 10 minutes.

7   Place the remaining butter in a saucepan and warm over medium-high heat. When the butter is melted, add the remaining brown sugar and salt and whisk until smooth.

Cook, stirring occasionally, until the brown sugar has dissolved. Slowly add the cream, while stirring constantly, until it has all been incorporated and the mixture is smooth. Reduce heat to low and simmer until the mixture starts to bubble. Remove from heat and stir in the lemon juice.

8   To serve, invert each cake into a bowl or onto a dish, spoon a generous amount of the sauce over each, and serve.

RHUBARB JAM

Place 4 cups chopped rhubarb, 1 cup water, ¾ cup sugar, and ½ teaspoon kosher salt in a saucepan and cook over high heat, stirring occasionally to prevent sticking, until nearly all of the liquid has evaporated. Add 1 teaspoon pectin and stir the mixture for 1 minute. Transfer to a sterilized mason jar and allow to cool completely before applying the lid and placing it in the refrigerator, where the jam will keep for up to 1 week.

STRAWBERRY RHUBARB RICOTTA CAKES

YIELD: **4 SERVINGS** / ACTIVE TIME: **30 MINUTES** / TOTAL TIME: **1 HOUR AND 15 MINUTES**

INGREDIENTS

1 stick of unsalted butter, at room temperature

½ cup sugar

2 eggs

¼ teaspoon pure vanilla extract

Zest of 1 lemon

¾ cup whole-milk ricotta cheese

¾ cup all-purpose flour

1 teaspoon baking powder

½ teaspoon kosher salt

½ cup minced strawberries, plus more for garnish

½ cup Rhubarb Jam (see sidebar)

1 cup whipped cream

1   Preheat the oven to 350°F and grease a 9 x 5–inch loaf pan. Place the butter and sugar in the work bowl of a stand mixer fitted with the paddle attachment and beat on high until the mixture is smooth and a pale yellow. Reduce speed to medium, add the eggs one at a time, and beat until incorporated. Add the vanilla, lemon zest, and ricotta and beat until the mixture is smooth.

2   Place the flour, baking powder, and salt in a mixing bowl and whisk to combine. Reduce the speed of the mixer to low, add the dry mixture to the wet mixture, and beat until incorporated. Scrape the mixing bowl as needed while mixing the batter.

3   Add the strawberries and fold to incorporate. Place the batter in the loaf pan, place it in the oven, and bake until a toothpick inserted into the center comes out clean, about 35 minutes. Remove from the oven and let cool to room temperature in the pan.

4   Remove the cooled cake from the pan and cut it into 8 equal pieces. Spread some of the jam over four of the pieces. Cover the jam with some of the whipped cream and then place the unadorned pieces of cake on top. Spread more whipped cream on top, garnish with additional strawberries, and serve.

CHAI-POACHED PEARS

YIELD: **4 SERVINGS** / ACTIVE TIME: **20 MINUTES** / TOTAL TIME: **1 HOUR AND 30 MINUTES**

INGREDIENTS

3 bags of chai tea

2 cinnamon sticks

4 whole cloves

2 teaspoons freshly grated nutmeg

½ cup sugar

4 ripe pears, left whole or peeled and sliced

1   Bring a saucepan of water to a boil. Add the tea bags, cinnamon sticks, cloves, and nutmeg, reduce the heat, and simmer for 10 minutes. Turn off the heat and let mixture steep for 30 minutes.

2   Remove the spices and tea bags from the water. Add the sugar and cook over low heat, while stirring, until the sugar is dissolved. Place the pears in the simmering tea and cook, while spooning the tea over the pears, until they are fork-tender, about 40 minutes. Turn the pears as they cook to ensure that they cook evenly.

3   Remove the pears from the tea, transfer them to the serving dishes, spoon some of the tea over the top, and serve.

BANANAS FOSTER

YIELD: **6 SERVINGS** / ACTIVE TIME: **10 MINUTES** / TOTAL TIME: **10 MINUTES**

INGREDIENTS

2 sticks of unsalted butter

1 cup firmly packed light brown sugar

6 bananas, cut lengthwise and halved

½ cup dark rum

¼ cup heavy cream

Vanilla ice cream, for serving

Cinnamon, to taste

1 Place a cast-iron skillet over medium-high heat and add the butter and brown sugar. Once the butter and sugar are melted, add the bananas to the pan and cook until they start to caramelize, about 3 minutes. Spoon the sauce over the bananas as they cook.

2 Remove the pan from heat, tilt it away from you, and add the rum. Using a long match or a long-handled lighter, carefully ignite the rum. Place the pan back over medium-high heat and shake the pan until the flames have gone out and the alcohol has cooked off. Add the cream and stir until the sauce has the desired texture and thickness.

3 Divide the bananas and sauce between the serving dishes. Top each portion with vanilla ice cream and cinnamon.

CHOCOLATE MOUSSE

YIELD: **6 SERVINGS** / ACTIVE TIME: **10 MINUTES** / TOTAL TIME: **1 HOUR AND 10 MINUTES**

INGREDIENTS

1 cup bittersweet chocolate chips

2 cups heavy cream, chilled

2 tablespoons sugar

3 egg whites

1 teaspoon pure vanilla extract

½ teaspoon fine sea salt

Whipped cream, for serving

1   Fill a small saucepan halfway with water and bring it to a gentle simmer. Place the chocolate chips in a heatproof bowl, place it over the simmering water, and stir until the chocolate is melted and smooth. Remove the chocolate from heat and set it aside.

2   Place the cream in a mixing bowl and beat until soft peaks form. Place the remaining ingredients in another bowl and beat until soft peaks form.

3   Gradually incorporate the melted chocolate into the egg white mixture and then gently fold in the cream.

4   Transfer the mousse into the serving dishes and refrigerate for at least 1 hour. To serve, top each portion with whipped cream.

CHOCOLATE-COVERED STRAWBERRIES

YIELD: **4 SERVINGS** / ACTIVE TIME: **10 MINUTES** / TOTAL TIME: **2 HOURS AND 10 MINUTES**

INGREDIENTS

2 pints of fresh strawberries

2 cups semisweet
chocolate chips

Graham cracker crumbs,
as needed

Finely ground almonds, as
needed

1 Rinse the strawberries well and pat them dry.

2 Fill a small saucepan halfway with water and bring it to a
gentle simmer. Place the chocolate chips in a heatproof
bowl, place it over the simmering water, and stir until the
chocolate is melted and smooth. Remove the bowl from
heat.

3 Dip each strawberry into the chocolate halfway, or
completely, whichever you prefer. Roll the coated
strawberries in graham cracker crumbs or ground
almonds. Line a baking sheet with parchment paper
and place the strawberries on the sheet. Place in the
refrigerator and chill for at least 2 hours before serving.

AFFOGATO

YIELD: **4 SERVINGS** / ACTIVE TIME: **5 MINUTES** / TOTAL TIME: **5 MINUTES**

INGREDIENTS

1 pint of vanilla ice cream

¼ cup Sambuca

1 teaspoon freshly
grated nutmeg

1¼ cups freshly brewed espresso
or very strong coffee

Whipped cream, for serving

1   Scoop ice cream into five small glasses. Pour some of the Sambuca over each scoop and sprinkle a bit of nutmeg on top.

2   Pour the espresso or coffee over the ice cream. Top each portion with whipped cream and serve.

SHORTBREAD

YIELD: **6 SERVINGS** / ACTIVE TIME: **20 MINUTES** / TOTAL TIME: **2 HOURS AND 30 MINUTES**

INGREDIENTS

2½ sticks of unsalted butter

10 tablespoons sugar

2½ cups all-purpose flour

1 teaspoon fine sea salt

1   Grate the butter into a mixing bowl and place it in the freezer for 30 minutes.

2   Preheat the oven to 325°F. Place ½ cup of the sugar, the flour, salt, and the frozen butter in the work bowl of a stand mixer fitted with the paddle attachment and beat on low until the mixture is fine like sand. Transfer the mixture to a greased round, 8-inch cake pan, place it in the oven, and bake until set and golden brown, about 1 hour and 15 minutes.

3   Remove from the oven, sprinkle the remaining sugar over the top, and let the shortbread cool before slicing it into rounds.

LEMON POSSET

YIELD: **6 SERVINGS** / ACTIVE TIME: **30 MINUTES** / TOTAL TIME: **4 HOURS**

INGREDIENTS

2 cups heavy cream

⅔ cup sugar

1 tablespoon lemon zest

6 tablespoons fresh lemon juice

1 cup whipped cream

Fresh blueberries, for serving

1. Place the heavy cream, sugar, and lemon zest in a saucepan and bring the mixture to a boil over medium heat, stirring constantly. Cook until the sugar has dissolved and the mixture has reduced slightly, about 10 minutes.

2. Remove the saucepan from heat and stir in the lemon juice. Let the mixture stand until a skin forms on the top, about 20 minutes. Strain the mixture through a fine sieve and transfer it to the refrigerator. Chill until set, about 3 hours.

3. About 10 minutes before you are ready to serve the posset, remove it from the refrigerator and let it come to room temperature. Cover the bottom of a serving dish with whipped cream and then alternate layers of the posset and whipped cream. Top each portion with a generous amount of blueberries and serve.

METRIC CONVERSION CHART

U.S. Measurement	Approximate Metric Liquid Measurement	Approximate Metric Dry Measurement
1 teaspoon	5 ml	–
1 tablespoon or ½ ounce	15 ml	14 g
1 ounce or ⅛ cup	30 ml	29 g
¼ cup or 2 ounces	60 ml	57 g
⅓ cup	80 ml	–
½ cup or 4 ounces	120 ml	113 g
⅔ cup	160 ml	–
¾ cup or 6 ounces	180 ml	–
1 cup or 8 ounces or ½ pint	240 ml	227 g
1½ cups or 12 ounces	350 ml	–
2 cups or 1 pint or 16 ounces	475 ml	454 g
3 cups or 1½ pints	700 ml	–
4 cups or 2 pints or 1 quart	950 ml	–

INDEX

ABOUT CIDER MILL PRESS BOOK PUBLISHERS

Good ideas ripen with time. From seed to harvest, Cider Mill Press brings fine reading, information, and entertainment together between the covers of its creatively crafted books. Our Cider Mill bears fruit twice a year, publishing a new crop of titles each spring and fall.

"Where Good Books Are Ready for Press"

VISIT US ONLINE AT
cidermillpress.com

OR WRITE TO US AT
PO Box 454
12 Spring St.
Kennebunkport, Maine 04046